# Financial Freedom

*Thru Miracle Of*

# S.I.P.

# Financial Freedom

*Thru Miracle Of*

# S.I.P.

**Mahesh Chandra Kaushik**

SEBI REGISTERED & NISM CERTIFIED
STOCK MARKET RESEARCH ANALYST

Ocean Books
Pvt. Ltd.

*Published by*
**Ocean Books (P) Ltd.**
4/19 Asaf Ali Road,
New Delhi-110 002 (INDIA)
e-mail: info@oceanbooks.in

ISBN 978-81-8430-639-2
**FINANCIAL FREEDOM THRU MIRACLE OF S.I.P.**
*by* Mahesh Chandra Kaushik

*Edition*
2024

*Price*
₹ 350.00 (Rupees Three Hundred Fifty only)



*Printed at*
SS Japan Arts, New Delhi

# Preface

Earning money is not a big deal or anything unusual; everyone is earning money. Stand next to a hawker in your area who is very popular just for a day. Then quietly note his turnover. For example, let's say he's a pani-puri hawker. He sells pani-puri for 11 hours a day from 9 in the morning to 8 in the evening. I ask you to visit his cart today and carry out an economic survey. Just go to his handcart and spend 10 minutes each at different times of the day. Collect financial samples as to how many customers visit the handcart in ten minutes from 9 to 12 in the morning and how much money he earned. It is not really his income; it is his turnover because he is also serving them the pani-puri.

In this way, you collect 6 samples of 10 minutes each at different times. This means you took out the average turnover of one hour, which will come to about 1000 to 3000 rupees. Now multiply this by 11 hours when his cart is open. You will get an idea of his full day's turnover, which will be around ₹ 10,000 to 30,000. He never takes leave or even if he does, it will be just a day or twoin a month. So, it means that his turnover for 30 days is approximately 3 lakh to 10 lakh rupees. What does this mean? If he is earning 1/4 profit on this turnover, then his monthly income is around 75,000 to 2,50,000 rupees. (This example is given with reference to the time of writing the book in 2021. Do adjust according to the time during which you read the book.)

You should not insist that a pani-puri seller cannot earn that much. This example does not represent every pani-puri seller. You have been asked to do the survey of the most famous and popular pani-puri seller in your city. My aim here is not to show a poor man as a rich one. You have to carry out the survey of a pani-puri seller whose sales, according to you, are the highest in your city.

You will be wondering whether you have bought a book on a pani puri seller or one on SIP. What kind of introduction is this? But don't worry, I am coming to the core of the book. My purpose for conducting such an economic survey is very simple. Now I will ask you to study the standard of living of that hawker his house, his living style, his clothes, his loans, etc. You'll see that based on his monthly average income of 1 lakh to 2 lakhs, he does not turn out be even 1/4 rich as he should have been.

## What is the reason of this?

The reason for this is that he knows how to earn money and conduct his business. He also has skill –you will not be able to make pani-puri like him at home. But he is completely ignorant about the basic rules of saving and increasing wealth. So, the book you have bought will give you practical information about the mentioned basic rules in detail.

In this book, I have also included the ancient secrets of wealth told to me by a Jain merchant. The basic theme of the book is to get financial freedom through SIP. But I've gone ahead and have tried to make it a complete encyclopaedia on Systematic Investment Plan, with the hope that my hard work can benefit millions of people in the coming years. If they understand my point and implement it in their lives, then even if they earn less money, they will be ten times richer. And if they can reach the ultimate goal, then they will be able to get financial freedom.

Here I have used the phrase 'the ultimate goal'. The reason is that, in practice, I give such advice to many people. But in most of the cases, I see that even before people have reached the goal of economic freedom, they are not able to handle the money that they have saved. They close the SIP or RD in the middle and indulge into alcoholism or other extravagances. Therefore, to get its full benefit, I advise you to respect money and avoid spending it on immoral activities like cigarettes, gutkha, alcoholism, gambling and the like.

To save one from going astray even before reaching the ultimate goal of financial freedom, Lakshmi – the goddess of wealth was worshipped in the Hindu religion. Money was given a sacred place, and it is considered an insult to Mother Lakshmi if it is spent on wrong things.

Not only in Hinduism, but also in Islam, there are rules for earning money, saving it and donating it. Islam also has a complete economics. I studied the laws of wealth of Hinduism as well as Islam and Christianity before writing the book because I do not give untested advice, just like Mahatma Gandhi. When I started writing 41 Tips for Success in Share Market, I was an investor and not a trader. I did not trade in intrade, options etc. So, how could I write a book on trading? Even if I did, would it benefit anyone? Therefore, despite being reminded several times by my publisher to write the book soon, before writing the book, I lived the life of a trader by trading in all segments of the market, including intraday and future options etc, for one whole year. Then based on experiences, I finally penned the book. Today, I am happy to see that the Hindi version and English translation of that book have been included in the bestseller books on trading. The Gujarati editions of all my books have also been published, much to my delight.

Now it's time to express gratitude. First of all, I am deeply grateful to the Sustainer of all, the Creator of the Universe, the Omnipotent, Omnipresent God (whom you may know as God, Allah, Ek Omkar, Satnam) who operates and destroys the universe, and who has given me the medium. This book has been created to show the right path to the common man.

I am also deeply grateful to my wife Seema Kaushik (of YouTube channel Seema's Kitchen fame) and my Gurudev Sri Sri 1008 Satyanarayanji Phalahari Baba. I have always received unwavering support for my work from my wife and spiritual protection from Gurudev.

Last but not the least, I would also like to convey my heartfelt gratitude to my 1.50 lakh followers, whose love helped me to complete this God-given work.

**– Mahesh Chandra Kaushik**
E-mail: mahesh2073@yahoo.com

# Contents

# 1

# Basic Information about SIP

Most of the readers might already be familiar with all the facts about what an SIP is, and what are the general benefits of SIP, etc. But when a book is written, it is very important to include the basic information about the subject so that it can be easily understood by all the categories of readers.

I request all the readers to read each chapter because no matter how knowledgeable one is, the possibility of getting some new information is endless. You can also get some new ideas from the initial information about an SIP:

The literal meaning of SIP is 'Systematic Investment Plan', ie, SIP is actually the short form of Systematic

Investment Plan. It means planning investment in a systematic manner.

SIP is widely used in Mutual Funds. Mutual Funds are a type of collective investment. In this, groups of investors invest in stocks or securities together.

In an SIP, a fixed amount is invested in a mutual fund at a fixed time interval, such as every month or every three months or every six months.

SIP has been found to be the safest, easiest and most profitable system among all the systems that have been discovered for investment in the world till date. Further in this book, you are going to learn how much power is hidden in this seemingly simple system.

In the olden times when mutual funds were not so popular, even middle-class people used to save money by SIP through recurring deposit accounts or RD.

SIP is also called the 'Dollar Cost Averaging' method. According to this, if you want to invest $1,000 in a share/ mutual fund unit and you have two options, either you invest all $1000 together or the second option lets you invest $10 in a month and invest $1000 in 100 months. If the market is down in this type of SIP investment, then you get more shares/units and if the market is up, then you get less shares/units. But from past experience, it is almost always seen that during the period of 100 months, ie, about nine years, you always stand to gain more profit than buying outright because firstly, you do not have to invest 1000 dollars at once. The remaining amount can be kept in fixed deposit. And during 9 years, you keep getting a good interest from it. Anyway, the only thing to keep in mind here is that Dollar Cost Averaging and Systematic Investment Plan work on the same principle.

## Summary

1. Most of the investment methods that have been discovered so far are based on SIP or Dollar Cost Averaging. Even my method of swing trading by averaging up to 9 times with Darvas Box theory uses the same technique.

2. SIP is the easiest and safest way to invest.

3. An SIP of a duration of at least 9 years is necessary to get or earn profit in the true sense and for proper comparative study. Real and effective benefits are visible in SIPs above 12 years.

4. If you do not have an urgent or a special need, then you should not discontinue the SIP plan before a period of 9 years.

# 2

# Nine Year long SIPs

After reading the previous chapter, you must be naturally curious that if the SIP is continued in an equity fund for at least 9 years, then what can be the estimated return? In fact, this benefit depends on which of your funds or in which scheme you have an SIP. The performance of different mutual fund managers and different schemes of mutual funds all vary.

But I always emphasise that you should choose a mutual fund scheme which has the highest AUM (Asset Under Management) or in other words, choose the mutual fund scheme with the largest size. You will ask, "Why so?" I will answer this question in the later chapters of this book as, at this point, it will be irrelevant. Right now, I just want to say that the example that I am going to give is of the HDFC Top 100 Fund Growth Plan. I have been working in the stock market since 2005. I remember that from 2007 to 2011, this fund was called HDFC Top 200. At that time, it was the fund with the highest AUM. That's why I thought it appropriate to choose this fund as an example.

Let us suppose a person wanted to invest approximately 10 lakh rupees for a period of 9 years. Then he had to invest ₹ 9259.25 per month in 108 months during 9 years through a SIP. We will check for two different time periods as to what would have happened if I had invested 10,80,000 in 108 months. We will take the rate of 10,000 per month for convenience.

1. For the first time period, we will assume that the SIP was started on 1st April 2008 and the maturity amount was taken after closing on 31st March 2017 after 9 years. This period has been chosen because there was a recession in the stock market in 2008 and there was a boom in the stock market in 2017. This is an ideal situation, wherein we will see what happened in the 9-year period.

2. For the second time period, we will assume that the SIP was started on 1st April, 2011 and closed on 31st March 2020 and the maturity amount was withdrawn. This is a serious adverse situation as the market remained almost stagnant from 2011 to 2103. Then the market remained bullish from

2014 to 2017. And from 2018 to 2020, the market phase was such that most of the small caps and mid-caps fell by 80%. On 31st March, 2020, due to the outbreak of the Corona virus (Covid-19), there was a worldwide recession, during which workers were forced to leave their homes. There was a lockdown and most of the industries had to be closed. So, we will see what is the return in such an unfavourable situation.

I have used the SIP calculator available on Moneycontrol.com website for calculation. In the first case, if we had invested 10,000 per month in HDFC Top 100 Growth Fund from 1st April 2008 to 31st March 2017, then after 9 years, on 31st March 2017 we would have received ₹ 20,84,165 against our original investment of ₹ 10,80,000. It has an annual rate of return of 14.34%. You can see its calculation sheet in Appendix-A given at the end of the book.

Now let's talk about the adverse situation. In the second case, if we look at the return for the period of 1st April 2011 to 31st March 2020, it would have given ₹ 16,00,543 on the original investment of 10,80,000 ie, 8.65% compounded return, which was not a very bad return despite the worldwide IT recession. I am providing the calculation which I found on moneycontrol.com. You can see its calculation sheet in Appendix-B at the end of the book.

I would like to summarise that the SIP of 9 years is an SIP of such duration; it is capable of giving returns even during times of recession.

## Summary

1. When the market conditions are good, a 9-year SIP can give an annual return of 12 to 20%.
2. Even when the market is bearish, a 9-year SIP can give 6 to 9% returns.
3. This period of 9 years is the minimum. Ideally, the SIP should be continued for 12 years.
4. Investing in the stock market and mutual funds is always subject to market risk. There is no guarantee of returns. But with a long-term SIP, the risk can be considerably reduced.
5. The worldwide recession of 2020 saw a decline of 30 to 50% in most investors' portfolios. Even then, there was some benefit in SIPs that were of a duration longer than 9 years.
6. Not all mutual fund schemes perform equally. Therefore, we should choose the largest mutual fund schemes for investment; the ones with the most asset management.

## APPENDIX-A

| | | | |
|---|---|---|---|
| Feb 01, 2016 | 10000 | 296.937 | 33.677 |
| Mar 01, 2016 | 10000 | 279.887 | 35.729 |
| Apr 01, 2016 | 10000 | 309.426 | 32.318 |
| May 02, 2016 | 10000 | 315.792 | 31.666 |
| Jun 01, 2016 | 10000 | 330.113 | 30.293 |
| Jul 01, 2016 | 10000 | 341.34 | 29.296 |
| Aug 01, 2016 | 10000 | 357.827 | 27.946 |
| Sep 01, 2016 | 10000 | 366.819 | 27.261 |
| Oct 03, 2016 | 10000 | 372.341 | 26.857 |
| Nov 01, 2016 | 10000 | 372.713 | 26.83 |
| Dec 01, 2016 | 10000 | 355.857 | 28.101 |
| Jan 02, 2017 | 10000 | 351.811 | 28.424 |
| Feb 01, 2017 | 10000 | 380.959 | 26.25 |
| Mar 01, 2017 | 10000 | 390.5 | 25.608 |

## APPENDIX-B

NAV as on Mar 31, 2017 344.774

Latest NAV 561.28100 (as on Jan 15, 2021)

| Investment Date | Investment Amount (Rs) | Purchase Price (Rs) | Units Purchased |
|---|---|---|---|
| Apr 01, 2011 | 10000 | 214.836 | 46.547 |
| May 02, 2011 | 10000 | 213.073 | 46.932 |
| Jun 01, 2011 | 10000 | 210.437 | 47.52 |
| Jul 01, 2011 | 10000 | 211.831 | 47.207 |
| Aug 01, 2011 | 10000 | 208.824 | 47.887 |
| Sep 02, 2011 | 10000 | 190.774 | 52.418 |
| Oct 03, 2011 | 10000 | 184.462 | 54.212 |
| Nov 01, 2011 | 10000 | 195.68 | 51.104 |
| Dec 01, 2011 | 10000 | 183.153 | 54.599 |
| Jan 02, 2012 | 10000 | 171.301 | 58.377 |
| Feb 01, 2012 | 10000 | 195.731 | 51.091 |

| Mar 01, 2012 | 10000 | 201.96 | 49.515 |
|---|---|---|---|
| Apr 02, 2012 | 10000 | 202.455 | 49.394 |
| May 02, 2012 | 10000 | 198.482 | 50.382 |
| Jun 01, 2012 | 10000 | 183.658 | 54.449 |
| Jul 02, 2012 | 10000 | 200.009 | 49.998 |
| Aug 01, 2012 | 10000 | 197.492 | 50.635 |
| Sep 03, 2012 | 10000 | 193.362 | 51.716 |
| Oct 01, 2012 | 10000 | 215.267 | 46.454 |
| Nov 01, 2012 | 10000 | 211.738 | 47.228 |
| Dec 03, 2012 | 10000 | 221.297 | 45.188 |
| Jan 01, 2013 | 10000 | 228.943 | 43.679 |
| Feb 01, 2013 | 10000 | 230.186 | 43.443 |
| Mar 01, 2013 | 10000 | 214.304 | 46.663 |
| Apr 01, 2013 | 10000 | 211.546 | 47.271 |
| May 02, 2013 | 10000 | 223.472 | 44.748 |
| Jun 03, 2013 | 10000 | 219.664 | 45.524 |
| Jul 01, 2013 | 10000 | 213.882 | 46.755 |
| Aug 01, 2013 | 10000 | 198.97 | 50.259 |
| Sep 02, 2013 | 10000 | 195.575 | 51.131 |
| Oct 01, 2013 | 10000 | 203.838 | 49.059 |
| Nov 01, 2013 | 10000 | 228.138 | 43.833 |
| Dec 02, 2013 | 10000 | 228.694 | 43.727 |
| Jan 01, 2014 | 10000 | 235.415 | 42.478 |
| Feb 03, 2014 | 10000 | 219.941 | 45.467 |
| Mar 03, 2014 | 10000 | 229.238 | 43.623 |
| Apr 01, 2014 | 10000 | 254.063 | 39.36 |
| May 02, 2014 | 10000 | 257.035 | 38.905 |
| Jun 02, 2014 | 10000 | 300.302 | 33.3 |
| Jul 01, 2014 | 10000 | 314.828 | 31.763 |
| Aug 01, 2014 | 10000 | 306.05 | 32.674 |
| Sep 01, 2014 | 10000 | 327.618 | 30.523 |
| Oct 01, 2014 | 10000 | 322.203 | 31.036 |

| | | | |
|---|---|---|---|
| Nov 03, 2014 | 10000 | 341.598 | 29.274 |
| Dec 01, 2014 | 10000 | 354.292 | 28.225 |
| Jan 01, 2015 | 10000 | 345.351 | 28.956 |
| Feb 02, 2015 | 10000 | 359.808 | 27.793 |
| Mar 02, 2015 | 10000 | 361.473 | 27.665 |
| Apr 01, 2015 | 10000 | 346.246 | 28.881 |
| May 04, 2015 | 10000 | 340.055 | 29.407 |
| Jun 01, 2015 | 10000 | 342.512 | 29.196 |
| Jul 01, 2015 | 10000 | 341.717 | 29.264 |
| Aug 03, 2015 | 10000 | 352.187 | 28.394 |
| Sep 01, 2015 | 10000 | 317.114 | 31.534 |
| Oct 01, 2015 | 10000 | 322.533 | 31.005 |
| Nov 02, 2015 | 10000 | 328.504 | 30.441 |
| Dec 01, 2015 | 10000 | 330.806 | 30.229 |
| Jan 01, 2016 | 10000 | 326.019 | 30.673 |
| Feb 01, 2016 | 10000 | 296.937 | 33.677 |
| Mar 01, 2016 | 10000 | 279.887 | 35.729 |
| Apr 01, 2016 | 10000 | 309.426 | 32.318 |
| May 02, 2016 | 10000 | 315.792 | 31.666 |
| Jun 01, 2016 | 10000 | 330.113 | 30.293 |
| Jul 01, 2016 | 10000 | 341.34 | 29.296 |
| Aug 01, 2016 | 10000 | 357.827 | 27.946 |
| Sep 01, 2016 | 10000 | 366.819 | 27.261 |
| Oct 03, 2016 | 10000 | 372.341 | 26.857 |
| Nov 01, 2016 | 10000 | 372.713 | 26.83 |
| Dec 01, 2016 | 10000 | 355.857 | 28.101 |
| Jan 02, 2017 | 10000 | 351.811 | 28.424 |
| Feb 01, 2017 | 10000 | 380.959 | 26.25 |
| Mar 01, 2017 | 10000 | 390.5 | 25.608 |
| Apr 03, 2017 | 10000 | 405.429 | 24.665 |
| May 02, 2017 | 10000 | 413.572 | 24.18 |
| Jun 01, 2017 | 10000 | 420.211 | 23.798 |
| Jul 03, 2017 | 10000 | 419.817 | 23.82 |

| | | | |
|---|---|---|---|
| Aug 01, 2017 | 10000 | 443.625 | 22.542 |
| Sep 01, 2017 | 10000 | 433.347 | 23.076 |
| Oct 03, 2017 | 10000 | 426.078 | 23.47 |
| Nov 01, 2017 | 10000 | 464.279 | 21.539 |
| Dec 01, 2017 | 10000 | 449.442 | 22.25 |
| Jan 01, 2018 | 10000 | 460.983 | 21.693 |
| Feb 01, 2018 | 10000 | 479.689 | 20.847 |
| Mar 01, 2018 | 10000 | 447.965 | 22.323 |
| Apr 02, 2018 | 10000 | 431.849 | 23.156 |
| May 02, 2018 | 10000 | 447.589 | 22.342 |
| Jun 01, 2018 | 10000 | 443.391 | 22.553 |
| Jul 02, 2018 | 10000 | 433.902 | 23.047 |
| Aug 01, 2018 | 10000 | 464.139 | 21.545 |
| Sep 03, 2018 | 10000 | 484.352 | 20.646 |
| Oct 01, 2018 | 10000 | 463.555 | 21.572 |
| Nov 01, 2018 | 10000 | 451.644 | 22.141 |
| Dec 03, 2018 | 10000 | 459.62 | 21.757 |
| Jan 01, 2019 | 10000 | 467.237 | 21.402 |
| Feb 01, 2019 | 10000 | 464.224 | 21.541 |
| Mar 01, 2019 | 10000 | 461.461 | 21.67 |
| Apr 01, 2019 | 10000 | 504.673 | 19.815 |
| May 02, 2019 | 10000 | 500.345 | 19.986 |
| Jun 03, 2019 | 10000 | 520.486 | 19.213 |
| Jul 01, 2019 | 10000 | 516.945 | 19.344 |
| Aug 01, 2019 | 10000 | 472.089 | 21.182 |
| Sep 03, 2019 | 10000 | 453.469 | 22.052 |
| Oct 01, 2019 | 10000 | 470.91 | 21.235 |
| Nov 01, 2019 | 10000 | 497.525 | 20.099 |
| Dec 02, 2019 | 10000 | 499.769 | 20.009 |
| Jan 01, 2020 | 10000 | 501.798 | 19.928 |
| Feb 03, 2020 | 10000 | 469.977 | 21.278 |
| Mar 02, 2020 | 10000 | 442.927 | 22.577 |

# 3

# Mutual Fund SIPs and Regular Monthly Income

Many investors keep looking for mutual funds that pay monthly dividends. There are also retired people who want regular monthly income from their deposits. There are also some mutual fund schemes that pay monthly dividends. But all these are debt-based schemes. That is, they are not stock market schemes but schemes investing in bonds of loans given to companies etc, in which the monthly return is less than the monthly interest received on the savings account of the banks. For this, I invented a method after a lot of hard work and research. This method was published in my blog Mutual Fund Genius in March 2019. I am going to explain this method of a regular source of monthly income to you in detail.

I also call it the golden egg laying hen, which keeps on giving golden eggs at regular monthly intervals. It is also worth mentioning here that if you invest in any product related to stocks, then you will always be at risk. But this monthly income system has a combination of three things:

- Lump sum investment
- SIP
- Systematic Withdrawal Plan

It has been calculated in such a way that it will be very difficult for it to *not* succeed. However, when there are situations like lockdowns or any other serious situation like a war, terror and panic is inevitable. As a result, a temporary decline may occur. But it is so systematic that it absorbs even such declines. A lot of my hard work has been invested in creating this. Since the past four years, my wife has invested in a Mutual Fund account in Axis Long Term Equity Fund. From this plan, she receives a regular monthly income-tax free income of ₹ 1000 without opting for any company pension plan. The profit on holding units also increases continuously. How is this happening?

Let's learn about this system:

1. Choose a good mutual fund scheme, whose AUM (Asset Under Management) is very large, one which has a track record of more than 5 years and which

is a diversified fund. You can get information about such schemes from my YouTube channel or from My Mutual Fund Genius Blog.

2. First of all, you have to invest a minimum lump sum of ₹ 1 lakh in this scheme. You can invest any amount in multiples of one lakh like 2 lakhs, 3 lakhs, 4 lakhs, 5 lakhs etc. as per your monthly income requirement. But my opinion is that if you have more money, then you should not put it in one scheme, rather invest it in different schemes in multiples of 1 lakh.

3. Now start an SIP of 2% of the lump sum invested amount in this fund. If there is a lump sum investment of 1 lakh, then the monthly SIP will be 2% of one lakh ie, ₹ 2000 per month.

4. Wait for at least one year. The SIP has to be continued after 1 year. But after one year, your tree will produce monthly fruits. After 1 year, you can withdraw 1% of the total value of your unit holding by selling the units. For example, after 1 year, your SIP of 1,00,000 basic and 12 months of 2000 per month was 24,000, ie, 1,24,000 in total. If the market value of the investment has become 1,60,000, then sell so many units that 1% amount of 1,60,000 will be received at ₹ 1,600. Then next month, check again to see your total unit value. Sell 1% of it and withdraw

the amount. In this way, you can sell 1% of the total unit value every month and take the amount home.

5. Now the question will arise whether after one year, should that 2% (2,000 per month) SIP be continued or stopped? So, the answer is that this SIP of 2,000 has to be continued as well. Now you will ask, "Are we stupid? We invest 2,000 per month and earn 1,600-1,700. What kind of strategy is this?"

   Actually, booking profit after 1 year is a very short time. Sometimes after a year, your portfolio may end up in loss due to a fall in the market. But I have also back-tested this method for 17 years. I will also provide the data and you can be rest assured that even after booking such monthly 1% profit, after approximately 4 years your monthly profit investment will exceed 2,000. If we look at the previous data, after 9 years, it goes even beyond 10,000 per month. If you can be patient for 4 years, that is, start booking 1% monthly profit after 4 years, then your original investment for 4 years will be 1,96,000. Naturally your portfolio being in profit would be above 2,00,000. Then your 1% monthly profit booking will be above the 2,000 monthly SIP investment and it will increase with time.

6. Let's take the example of my wife's account given above. She first made a lump-sum investment of

around 1 lakh in Axis Long Term Equity Fund. Then she continued the SIP of 1000 rupees per month for 3 years. After 4 years, she thought, 'Why bother to withdraw 1% of the fund value every month?' So, she directly started Systematic Withdrawal Plan of ₹ 2,000 per month. That is, ₹ 1000 is invested in SIP on the 5th of every month and she withdraws ₹ 2,000 every month on the 20th of the month. It is considered to be a unit sold 4 years ago and does not attract income tax. The overall savings is 1000 per month. Now her fund value has crossed 3 lakhs. So, now she is going to withdraw ₹ 3,000 per month. So, the monthly SIP will remain ₹ 1,000, but the unit purchased today will continue to grow. Monthly withdrawals should not exceed 1% of the total fund value. It will take her 100 months ie, more than 8 years to withdraw the entire fund. Till then the SIP of 1,000 per month that is in operation will increase the fund value. Hence, the chances of regular income shutting down in the system are very low.

7. For those who still have little understanding of this method, I will summarize the points once again. After investing a lump sum amount in a good diversified mutual fund, opt for SIP of a certain amount per month in that fund. If you have made a lump sum investment of one lakh then this SIP should be of 2,000 per month. Accordingly, on the

basis of your lump sum investment, you can decide your SIP. For example, if you invest a lump sum of 5 lakhs, then SIP should be ₹ 10,000 per month. Now wait 1 to 4 years. After that, instead of checking the market value of your portfolio every month, check it once a year in the month of January. Suppose you invest a lump sum of 1 lakh and start an SIP of 2,000 per month, and after 4 years this value comes to 3,64,325, then 1% of it is 3,643.25. So, you put in a systematic withdrawal plan of ₹ 3600 per month for that year. That is, by selling your old unit every month, you will continue to get ₹ 3,600 monthly. Your SIP of 2000 per month will continue. It is a new investment whose profit booking number will appear after about 100 months because you are withdrawing only 1% of the amount per month. So, for the next 100 months (about 8 years) the 2000 rupees will remain invested. Now check the market value of your investment again in January next year. Suppose now it comes to 4,34,256. So, for that year, you keep on selling units and get an amount equal to about 1% of it ie, ₹ 4,300 per month.

8. If you still haven't quite understood, then I will provide you with practical data. I have back-tested this method on the data of the HDFC Top 200 Fund G Plan from 1st April, 1999 to 1st March, 2016 which

is provided to you in Appendix 'C'. Only after going through Appendix Sheet C, you will get an accurate idea of its strength. You will see that the total investment made in 17 years is 5,08,000, which includes 1,00,000 as the initial investment and 2,000 monthly SIP. But by selling units at 1% per month, the long-term capital gain was ₹ 13,98,879. Even after 17 years, the holding had a net profit of ₹ 4,13,527 and after 17 years, one was getting a monthly income of approximately ₹ 10,000 per month as well. Isn't that a great deal? You can check its calculation sheet in Appendix-C given at the end of the book.

## Summary

1. By mixing the lump sum investment and systematic withdrawal plan with the SIP, we can create a system of tax free (long term capital gains) monthly income system.

2. Here the SIP is to be done per month equal to 2% of the lump sum investment and 1% of the unit value is to be sold every month to make profit or long term capital gain.

3. If you want, you can start after 1 year by selling as much as 1% of the total unit value per month.

But, ideally, units should be sold after 4 years for an amount equal to 1% per month.

4. Like any investment based on the stock market, there is market risk involved. But being a disciplined long-term system, the risk in this is comparatively very less.

5. If you have understood this system and are getting excited after reading the initial chapters, then you must tell me your thoughts by reviewing the book.

❑

# APPENDIX-C

| Investment Date | Investment | NAV | Units Purchased | total units in folio | total investment at cost | total fund value at NAV | net profit/loss | Redumption | Monthly Income |
|---|---|---|---|---|---|---|---|---|---|
| 01-Mar-99 | 1,00,000 | 13.54 | 7385.524372 | 7385.524372 | 100000 | 100000 | 0 | | 0 |
| 01-Apr-99 | 2000 | 14.49 | 138.026225 | 7523.550597 | 102000 | 109016.2482 | 7016.248154 | 0 | 0 |
| 03-May-99 | 2000 | 13.36 | 149.7005988 | 7673.251196 | 104000 | 102514.636 | -1485.364021 | 0 | 0 |
| 01-Jun-99 | 2000 | 14.42 | 138.6962552 | 7811.947451 | 106000 | 112648.2822 | 6648.282247 | 0 | 0 |
| 01-Jul-99 | 2000 | 14.43 | 138.6001386 | 7950.54759 | 108000 | 114726.4017 | 6726.401721 | 0 | 0 |
| 02-Aug-99 | 2000 | 16.51 | 121.1387038 | 8071.686294 | 110000 | 133263.5407 | 23263.54071 | 0 | 0 |
| 01-Sep-99 | 2000 | 18.39 | 108.754758 | 8180.441052 | 112000 | 150438.3109 | 38438.31094 | 0 | 0 |
| 01-Oct-99 | 2000 | 18.94 | 105.5966209 | 8286.037673 | 114000 | 156937.5535 | 42937.55352 | 0 | 0 |
| 01-Nov-99 | 2000 | 16.32 | 122.5490196 | 8408.586692 | 116000 | 137228.1348 | 21228.13482 | 0 | 0 |
| 01-Dec-99 | 2000 | 18.4 | 108.6956522 | 8517.282344 | 118000 | 156717.9951 | 38717.99514 | 0 | 0 |
| 03-Jan-00 | 2000 | 21.68 | 92.25092251 | 8609.533267 | 120000 | 186654.6812 | 66654.68123 | 0 | 0 |
| 01-Feb-00 | 2000 | 22.11 | 90.45680687 | 8699.990074 | 122000 | 192356.7805 | 70356.78053 | 0 | 0 |
| 01-Mar-00 | 2000 | 24.32 | 82.23684211 | 8782.226916 | 124000 | 213583.7586 | 89583.75859 | 0 | 0 |
| 03-Apr-00 | 2000 | 20.85 | 95.92326139 | 8878.150177 | 126000 | 185109.4312 | 59109.4312 | 88.77697842 | 1851 |
| 02-May-00 | 2000 | 15.7 | 127.388535 | 8916.761734 | 128000 | 139993.1592 | 11993.15922 | 89.17197452 | 1400 |
| 01-Jun-00 | 2000 | 15.7 | 127.388535 | 8954.978294 | 130000 | 140593.1592 | 10593.15922 | 89.55414013 | 1406 |
| 03-Jul-00 | 2000 | 17.4 | 114.9425287 | 8980.366683 | 132000 | 156258.3803 | 24258.38028 | 89.82758621 | 1563 |
| 01-Aug-00 | 2000 | 15.33 | 130.4631442 | 9021.002241 | 134000 | 138291.9644 | 4291.964353 | 90.21526419 | 1383 |
| 04-Sep-00 | 2000 | 16.7 | 119.760479 | 9050.547456 | 136000 | 151144.1425 | 15144.14251 | 90.47904192 | 1511 |
| 03-Oct-00 | 2000 | 14.28 | 140.0560224 | 9100.124436 | 138000 | 129949.7769 | -8050.22305 | 90.96638655 | 1299 |
| 01-Nov-00 | 2000 | 13.93 | 143.5750179 | 9152.733068 | 140000 | 127497.5716 | -12502.42837 | 91.52907394 | 1275 |
| 01-Dec-00 | 2000 | 14.98 | 133.5113485 | 9194.715342 | 142000 | 137736.8358 | -4263.164174 | 91.92256342 | 1377 |
| 01-Jan-01 | 2000 | 15.26 | 131.061599 | 9233.854378 | 144000 | 140908.6178 | -3091.382196 | 92.33289646 | 1409 |
| 01-Feb-01 | 2000 | 15.67 | 127.6324186 | 9269.1539 | 146000 | 145247.6416 | -752.3583889 | 92.66113593 | 1452 |
| 01-Mar-01 | 2000 | 16.12 | 124.0694789 | 9300.562243 | 148000 | 149925.0634 | 1925.063355 | 92.99007444 | 1499 |
| 02-Apr-01 | 2000 | 13.28 | 150.6024096 | 9358.174578 | 150000 | 124276.5584 | -25723.4416 | 93.59939759 | 1243 |
| 02-May-01 | 2000 | 14.19 | 140.944327 | 9405.519507 | 152000 | 133464.3218 | -18535.67819 | 94.08033827 | 1335 |
| 01-Jun-01 | 2000 | 14.34 | 139.4700139 | 9450.909183 | 154000 | 135526.0377 | -18473.96231 | 94.49093445 | 1355 |
| 02-Jul-01 | 2000 | 13.57 | 147.3839352 | 9503.802184 | 156000 | 128966.5956 | -27033.40437 | 95.06263817 | 1290 |
| 01-Aug-01 | 2000 | 13.16 | 151.9756839 | 9560.71523 | 158000 | 125819.0124 | -32180.98758 | 95.59270517 | 1258 |
| 03-Sep-01 | 2000 | 13.15 | 152.0912548 | 9617.213779 | 160000 | 126466.3612 | -33533.6388 | 96.19771863 | 1265 |
| 01-Oct-01 | 2000 | 11.71 | 170.794193 | 9691.810254 | 162000 | 113491.0981 | -48508.90193 | 96.92570453 | 1135 |

| | | | | | | | | | |
|---|---|---|---|---|---|---|---|---|---|
| 01-Nov-01 | 2000 | 12.88 | 155.2795031 | 9750.164052 | 164000 | 125582.113 | -38417.88701 | 97.51552795 | 1256 |
| 03-Dec-01 | 2000 | 13.8 | 144.9275362 | 9797.57606 | 166000 | 135206.5496 | -30793.45037 | 97.97101449 | 1352 |
| 01-Jan-02 | 2000 | 13.57 | 147.3839352 | 9846.988981 | 168000 | 133623.6405 | -34376.35953 | 98.45246868 | 1336 |
| 01-Feb-02 | 2000 | 14.73 | 135.7773252 | 9884.313838 | 170000 | 145595.9428 | -24404.05717 | 98.84589274 | 1456 |
| 01-Mar-02 | 2000 | 16.48 | 121.3592233 | 9906.827168 | 172000 | 163264.5117 | -8735.48827 | 99.08980583 | 1633 |
| 01-Apr-02 | 2000 | 16.93 | 118.1334908 | 9925.870853 | 174000 | 168044.9935 | -5955.006457 | 99.23213231 | 1680 |
| 02-May-02 | 2000 | 16.9 | 118.3431953 | 9944.981916 | 176000 | 168070.1944 | -7929.805618 | 99.46745562 | 1681 |
| 03-Jun-02 | 2000 | 15.9 | 125.7861635 | 9971.300624 | 178000 | 158543.6799 | -19456.32008 | 99.68553459 | 1585 |
| 01-Jul-02 | 2000 | 16.5 | 121.2121212 | 9992.827211 | 180000 | 164881.649 | -15118.35103 | 99.93939394 | 1649 |
| 01-Aug-02 | 2000 | 15.55 | 128.6173633 | 10021.50518 | 182000 | 155834.4055 | -26165.59445 | 100.192926 | 1558 |
| 02-Sep-02 | 2000 | 16.37 | 122.1747098 | 10043.48696 | 184000 | 164411.8816 | -19588.1184 | 100.4276115 | 1644 |
| 01-Oct-02 | 2000 | 14.9 | 134.2281879 | 10077.28754 | 186000 | 150151.5843 | -35848.41565 | 100.8053691 | 1502 |
| 01-Nov-02 | 2000 | 15.29 | 130.8044474 | 10107.28662 | 188000 | 154540.4124 | -33459.5876 | 101.0464356 | 1545 |
| 02-Dec-02 | 2000 | 16.57 | 120.7000604 | 10126.94024 | 190000 | 167803.3998 | -22196.60017 | 101.2673506 | 1678 |
| 01-Jan-03 | 2000 | 17.36 | 115.2073733 | 10140.88027 | 192000 | 176045.6814 | -15954.31858 | 101.3824885 | 1760 |
| 03-Feb-03 | 2000 | 17.34 | 115.3402537 | 10154.83803 | 194000 | 176084.8915 | -17915.10854 | 101.5570934 | 1761 |
| 03-Mar-03 | 2000 | 17.58 | 113.7656428 | 10167.04658 | 196000 | 178736.6789 | -17263.32112 | 101.6496018 | 1787 |
| 01-Apr-03 | 2000 | 16.71 | 119.6888091 | 10185.08579 | 198000 | 170192.7835 | -27807.21649 | 101.8551765 | 1702 |
| 02-May-03 | 2000 | 17.64 | 113.3786848 | 10196.6093 | 200000 | 179868.188 | -20131.81202 | 101.984127 | 1799 |
| 02-Jun-03 | 2000 | 20.84 | 95.96928983 | 10190.59446 | 202000 | 212371.9885 | 10371.98852 | 101.9193858 | 2124 |
| 01-Jul-03 | 2000 | 23.057 | 86.74155354 | 10175.41663 | 204000 | 234614.5812 | 30614.58116 | 101.7478423 | 2346 |
| 01-Aug-03 | 2000 | 24.408 | 81.94034743 | 10155.60913 | 206000 | 247878.1077 | 41878.10769 | 101.5650606 | 2479 |
| 01-Sep-03 | 2000 | 29.168 | 68.56829402 | 10122.61237 | 208000 | 295256.3575 | 87256.35747 | 101.2410861 | 2953 |
| 01-Oct-03 | 2000 | 30.215 | 66.1922886 | 10087.56357 | 210000 | 304795.7332 | 94795.73319 | 100.8770478 | 3048 |
| 03-Nov-03 | 2000 | 33.876 | 59.03884756 | 10045.72537 | 212000 | 340308.9925 | 128308.9925 | 100.4545991 | 3403 |
| 01-Dec-03 | 2000 | 35.192 | 56.83109798 | 10002.10187 | 214000 | 351993.9689 | 137993.9689 | 100.0227324 | 3520 |
| 01-Jan-04 | 2000 | 41.043 | 48.72938138 | 9950.808515 | 216000 | 408411.0339 | 192411.0339 | 99.50539678 | 4084 |
| 03-Feb-04 | 2000 | 38.825 | 51.51320026 | 9902.816319 | 218000 | 384476.8436 | 166476.8436 | 99.0341275 | 3845 |
| 01-Mar-04 | 2000 | 40.865 | 48.9416371 | 9852.723828 | 220000 | 402631.5592 | 182631.5592 | 98.51951548 | 4026 |
| 01-Apr-04 | 2000 | 41.106 | 48.65469761 | 9802.85901 | 222000 | 402956.3225 | 180956.3225 | 98.03921569 | 4030 |
| 03-May-04 | 2000 | 41.075 | 48.69141814 | 9753.511213 | 224000 | 400625.4731 | 176625.4731 | 97.52891053 | 4006 |
| 01-Jun-04 | 2000 | 35.633 | 56.12774675 | 9712.110049 | 226000 | 346071.6174 | 120071.6174 | 97.12906575 | 3461 |
| 01-Jul-04 | 2000 | 36.701 | 54.49442794 | 9669.475411 | 228000 | 354879.4171 | 126879.4171 | 96.70036239 | 3549 |
| 02-Aug-04 | 2000 | 38.849 | 51.48137661 | 9624.256425 | 230000 | 373892.7379 | 143892.7379 | 96.24443358 | 3739 |

| | | | | | | | | | |
|---|---|---|---|---|---|---|---|---|---|
| 01-Sep-04 | 2000 | 40.019 | 49.97626128 | 9577.988253 | 232000 | 383301.5119 | 151301.5119 | 95.77950474 | 3833 |
| 01-Oct-04 | 2000 | 42.931 | 46.5863828 | 9528.795131 | 234000 | 409080.7038 | 175080.7038 | 95.29244602 | 4091 |
| 01-Nov-04 | 2000 | 43.397 | 46.08613499 | 9479.58882 | 236000 | 411385.716 | 175385.716 | 94.79917967 | 4114 |
| 01-Dec-04 | 2000 | 47.125 | 42.4403183 | 9427.229959 | 238000 | 444258.2118 | 206258.2118 | 94.28116711 | 4443 |
| 03-Jan-05 | 2000 | 52.294 | 38.24530539 | 9371.194097 | 240000 | 490057.2241 | 250057.2241 | 93.72012086 | 4901 |
| 01-Feb-05 | 2000 | 50.394 | 39.68726436 | 9317.161241 | 242000 | 469529.0236 | 227529.0236 | 93.16585308 | 4695 |
| 01-Mar-05 | 2000 | 52.786 | 37.88883416 | 9261.884222 | 244000 | 488897.8205 | 244897.8205 | 92.61925511 | 4889 |
| 01-Apr-05 | 2000 | 53.222 | 37.578445 | 9206.843412 | 246000 | 490006.6201 | 244006.6201 | 92.06719026 | 4900 |
| 02-May-05 | 2000 | 50.255 | 39.79703512 | 9154.573256 | 248000 | 460063.079 | 212063.079 | 91.5530793 | 4601 |
| 01-Jun-05 | 2000 | 54.973 | 36.38149637 | 9099.401673 | 250000 | 500221.4082 | 250221.4082 | 90.99012242 | 5002 |
| 01-Jul-05 | 2000 | 57.492 | 34.78744869 | 9043.199 | 252000 | 519911.5969 | 267911.5969 | 90.42997287 | 5199 |
| 01-Aug-05 | 2000 | 60.918 | 32.83101875 | 8985.600046 | 254000 | 547384.7836 | 293384.7836 | 89.85849831 | 5474 |
| 01-Sep-05 | 2000 | 64.253 | 31.12695127 | 8926.868499 | 256000 | 573578.0816 | 317578.0816 | 89.27209624 | 5736 |
| 03-Oct-05 | 2000 | 70.553 | 28.34748345 | 8865.943886 | 258000 | 625518.939 | 367518.939 | 88.6567545 | 6255 |
| 02-Nov-05 | 2000 | 66.878 | 29.90520051 | 8807.192332 | 260000 | 589007.4088 | 329007.4088 | 88.07081551 | 5890 |
| 01-Dec-05 | 2000 | 75.162 | 26.60919081 | 8745.730707 | 262000 | 657346.6114 | 395346.6114 | 87.45110561 | 6573 |
| 02-Jan-06 | 2000 | 79.874 | 25.03943711 | 8683.319039 | 264000 | 693571.4249 | 429571.4249 | 86.83676791 | 6936 |
| 01-Feb-06 | 2000 | 84.001 | 23.80924037 | 8620.291511 | 266000 | 724113.1072 | 458113.1072 | 86.20135475 | 7241 |
| 01-Mar-06 | 2000 | 89.277 | 22.40218645 | 8556.492343 | 268000 | 763897.9669 | 495897.9669 | 85.56515116 | 7639 |
| 03-Apr-06 | 2000 | 98.486 | 20.30745487 | 8491.234647 | 270000 | 836267.7354 | 566267.7354 | 84.91562253 | 8363 |
| 02-May-06 | 2000 | 101.43 | 19.71803214 | 8426.037056 | 272000 | 854652.9386 | 582652.9386 | 84.26501035 | 8547 |
| 01-Jun-06 | 2000 | 84.905 | 23.55573877 | 8365.327785 | 274000 | 710258.1555 | 436258.1555 | 83.65820623 | 7103 |
| 03-Jul-06 | 2000 | 86.3 | 23.17497103 | 8304.844549 | 276000 | 716708.0846 | 440708.0846 | 83.04750869 | 7167 |
| 01-Aug-06 | 2000 | 87.295 | 22.91081963 | 8244.70786 | 278000 | 719721.7727 | 441721.7727 | 82.44458446 | 7197 |
| 01-Sep-06 | 2000 | 96.306 | 20.76713808 | 8183.030414 | 280000 | 788074.927 | 508074.927 | 81.83290761 | 7881 |
| 03-Oct-06 | 2000 | 100.218 | 19.95649484 | 8121.154001 | 282000 | 813885.8117 | 531885.8117 | 81.21295576 | 8139 |
| 01-Nov-06 | 2000 | 105.66 | 18.92863903 | 8058.869684 | 284000 | 851500.1709 | 567500.1709 | 80.58868067 | 8515 |
| 01-Dec-06 | 2000 | 110.994 | 18.01899202 | 7996.299996 | 286000 | 887541.3217 | 601541.3217 | 79.95927708 | 8875 |
| 02-Jan-07 | 2000 | 110.855 | 18.04158586 | 7934.382305 | 288000 | 879565.9504 | 591565.9504 | 79.34689459 | 8796 |
| 01-Feb-07 | 2000 | 113.266 | 17.65754949 | 7872.692959 | 290000 | 891708.4407 | 601708.4407 | 78.72618438 | 8917 |
| 01-Mar-07 | 2000 | 104.794 | 19.08506212 | 7813.051837 | 292000 | 818760.9542 | 526760.9542 | 78.13424433 | 8188 |
| 02-Apr-07 | 2000 | 100.009 | 19.99820016 | 7754.915793 | 294000 | 775561.3735 | 481561.3735 | 77.55302023 | 7756 |
| 03-May-07 | 2000 | 113.528 | 17.61679938 | 7694.979572 | 296000 | 873595.6409 | 577595.6409 | 76.95017969 | 8736 |
| 01-Jun-07 | 2000 | 119.524 | 16.73304106 | 7634.762434 | 298000 | 912537.3451 | 614537.3451 | 76.34449985 | 9125 |

| | | | | | | | | | |
|---|---|---|---|---|---|---|---|---|---|
| 02-Jul-07 | 2000 | 121.292 | 16.48913356 | 7574.907067 | 300000 | 918775.628 | 618775.628 | 75.75108004 | 9188 |
| 01-Aug-07 | 2000 | 122.866 | 16.27789624 | 7515.433884 | 302000 | 923391.2995 | 621391.2995 | 75.15504696 | 9234 |
| 03-Sep-07 | 2000 | 127.093 | 15.73650791 | 7456.015344 | 304000 | 947607.3582 | 643607.3582 | 74.55957448 | 9476 |
| 01-Oct-07 | 2000 | 141.248 | 14.15949252 | 7395.615263 | 306000 | 1044615.865 | 738615.8646 | 73.95502945 | 10446 |
| 01-Nov-07 | 2000 | 159.7 | 12.52348153 | 7334.183715 | 308000 | 1171269.139 | 863269.1392 | 73.34376957 | 11713 |
| 03-Dec-07 | 2000 | 160.418 | 12.46742834 | 7273.307374 | 310000 | 1166769.422 | 856769.4223 | 72.73497987 | 11668 |
| 01-Jan-08 | 2000 | 170.241 | 11.74805129 | 7212.320445 | 312000 | 1227832.645 | 915832.6449 | 72.12128688 | 12278 |
| 01-Feb-08 | 2000 | 151.276 | 13.22086732 | 7153.420026 | 314000 | 1082140.768 | 768140.7679 | 71.53150533 | 10821 |
| 03-Mar-08 | 2000 | 141.867 | 14.09771124 | 7095.986232 | 316000 | 1006686.279 | 690686.2788 | 70.96082951 | 10067 |
| 01-Apr-08 | 2000 | 130.829 | 15.28713053 | 7040.312533 | 318000 | 921077.0484 | 603077.0484 | 70.40487965 | 9211 |
| 02-May-08 | 2000 | 145.16 | 13.77790025 | 6983.685554 | 320000 | 1013751.795 | 693751.795 | 69.84017636 | 10138 |
| 02-Jun-08 | 2000 | 135.425 | 14.76832195 | 6928.613699 | 322000 | 938307.5102 | 616307.5102 | 69.28558243 | 9383 |
| 01-Jul-08 | 2000 | 111.825 | 17.88508831 | 6877.213205 | 324000 | 769044.3667 | 445044.3667 | 68.76816454 | 7690 |
| 01-Aug-08 | 2000 | 126.743 | 15.77996418 | 6824.225005 | 326000 | 864922.7498 | 538922.7498 | 68.24045509 | 8649 |
| 01-Sep-08 | 2000 | 129.16 | 15.48467018 | 6771.46922 | 328000 | 874602.9645 | 546602.9645 | 67.71446268 | 8746 |
| 01-Oct-08 | 2000 | 120.227 | 16.63519842 | 6720.389956 | 330000 | 807972.3232 | 477972.3232 | 67.2062016 | 8080 |
| 03-Nov-08 | 2000 | 95.928 | 20.84897006 | 6674.032724 | 332000 | 640226.6112 | 308226.6112 | 66.73755316 | 6402 |
| 01-Dec-08 | 2000 | 84.587 | 23.64429522 | 6630.939466 | 334000 | 560891.2766 | 226891.2766 | 66.31042595 | 5609 |
| 01-Jan-09 | 2000 | 94.479 | 21.16872533 | 6585.797766 | 336000 | 622219.5871 | 286219.5871 | 65.85590449 | 6222 |
| 02-Feb-09 | 2000 | 85.752 | 23.32307118 | 6543.264932 | 338000 | 561098.0545 | 223098.0545 | 65.4328762 | 5611 |
| 02-Mar-09 | 2000 | 82.213 | 24.3270529 | 6502.159109 | 340000 | 534562.0068 | 194562.0068 | 65.0262124 | 5346 |
| 01-Apr-09 | 2000 | 93.541 | 21.38099871 | 6458.513895 | 342000 | 604135.8483 | 262135.8483 | 64.58130659 | 6041 |
| 04-May-09 | 2000 | 113.162 | 17.67377742 | 6411.606366 | 344000 | 725550.1996 | 381550.1996 | 64.12046447 | 7256 |
| 01-Jun-09 | 2000 | 140.372 | 14.2478557 | 6361.733757 | 346000 | 893009.291 | 547009.291 | 63.61667569 | 8930 |
| 01-Jul-09 | 2000 | 145.276 | 13.76689837 | 6311.883981 | 348000 | 916965.2572 | 568965.2572 | 63.12123131 | 9170 |
| 03-Aug-09 | 2000 | 158.221 | 12.64054738 | 6261.403296 | 350000 | 990685.4909 | 640685.4909 | 62.61494998 | 9907 |
| 01-Sep-09 | 2000 | 157.155 | 12.72628933 | 6211.514636 | 352000 | 976170.5826 | 624170.5826 | 62.11701823 | 9762 |
| 01-Oct-09 | 2000 | 171.852 | 11.637921 | 6161.035538 | 354000 | 1058786.279 | 704786.2793 | 61.61115378 | 10588 |
| 03-Nov-09 | 2000 | 162.803 | 12.28478591 | 6111.709171 | 356000 | 995004.5881 | 639004.5881 | 61.11680989 | 9950 |
| 01-Dec-09 | 2000 | 178.983 | 11.1742455 | 6061.766606 | 358000 | 1084953.172 | 726953.1725 | 60.62028237 | 10850 |
| 04-Jan-10 | 2000 | 181.428 | 11.02365677 | 6012.169981 | 360000 | 1090775.975 | 730775.9752 | 60.12302401 | 10908 |
| 01-Feb-10 | 2000 | 173.925 | 11.49920943 | 5963.546166 | 362000 | 1037209.767 | 675209.7669 | 59.6349001 | 10372 |
| 02-Mar-10 | 2000 | 176.554 | 11.32797898 | 5915.239245 | 364000 | 1044359.15 | 680359.1497 | 59.15470621 | 10444 |
| 01-Apr-10 | 2000 | 184.923 | 10.81531232 | 5866.899851 | 366000 | 1084924.721 | 718924.7212 | 58.66766168 | 10849 |
| 03-May-10 | 2000 | 186.819 | 10.70554922 | 5818.937739 | 368000 | 1087088.129 | 719088.1294 | 58.19001279 | 10871 |

| | | | | | | | | | |
|---|---|---|---|---|---|---|---|---|---|
| 01-Jun-10 | 2000 | 181.953 | 10.99184954 | 5771.739575 | 370000 | 1050185.331 | 680185.331 | 57.71820195 | 10502 |
| 01-Jul-10 | 2000 | 192.971 | 10.36425162 | 5724.385625 | 372000 | 1104640.418 | 732640.4184 | 57.24176172 | 11046 |
| 02-Aug-10 | 2000 | 201.717 | 9.914880749 | 5677.058744 | 374000 | 1145159.259 | 771159.2587 | 56.77260717 | 11452 |
| 01-Sep-10 | 2000 | 207.327 | 9.646596922 | 5629.932734 | 376000 | 1167237.064 | 791237.0639 | 56.29753964 | 11672 |
| 01-Oct-10 | 2000 | 227.948 | 8.773930897 | 5582.409125 | 378000 | 1272498.995 | 894498.9952 | 55.82413533 | 12725 |
| 01-Nov-10 | 2000 | 229.976 | 8.696559641 | 5535.281549 | 380000 | 1272981.91 | 892981.9096 | 55.35360212 | 12730 |
| 01-Dec-10 | 2000 | 226.017 | 8.848891898 | 5488.776839 | 382000 | 1240556.875 | 858556.8749 | 54.88967644 | 12406 |
| 03-Jan-11 | 2000 | 226.586 | 8.826670668 | 5442.713833 | 384000 | 1233242.757 | 849242.7567 | 54.42525134 | 12332 |
| 01-Feb-11 | 2000 | 202.436 | 9.879665672 | 5398.168248 | 386000 | 1092783.587 | 706783.5874 | 53.98249323 | 10928 |
| 01-Mar-11 | 2000 | 204.031 | 9.802431983 | 5353.988186 | 388000 | 1092379.564 | 704379.5637 | 53.54088349 | 10924 |
| 01-Apr-11 | 2000 | 214.836 | 9.309426726 | 5309.75673 | 390000 | 1140726.897 | 750726.8968 | 53.09631533 | 11407 |
| 02-May-11 | 2000 | 213.073 | 9.386454408 | 5266.046869 | 392000 | 1122052.404 | 730052.4045 | 52.66270245 | 11221 |
| 01-Jun-11 | 2000 | 210.437 | 9.504032086 | 5222.888198 | 394000 | 1099088.924 | 705088.9238 | 52.22940833 | 10991 |
| 01-Jul-11 | 2000 | 211.831 | 9.441488734 | 5180.100279 | 396000 | 1097305.822 | 701305.8222 | 51.80072794 | 10973 |
| 01-Aug-11 | 2000 | 208.824 | 9.577443206 | 5137.876994 | 398000 | 1072912.025 | 674912.0254 | 51.37819408 | 10729 |
| 02-Sep-11 | 2000 | 190.774 | 10.48360888 | 5096.982409 | 400000 | 972371.7221 | 572371.7221 | 50.97130636 | 9724 |
| 03-Oct-11 | 2000 | 184.462 | 10.84234151 | 5056.853444 | 402000 | 932797.3 | 530797.3 | 50.56868081 | 9328 |
| 01-Nov-11 | 2000 | 195.68 | 10.2207686 | 5016.505532 | 404000 | 981629.8025 | 577629.8025 | 50.1635323 | 9816 |
| 01-Dec-11 | 2000 | 183.153 | 10.91983205 | 4977.261832 | 406000 | 911600.4362 | 505600.4362 | 49.7725945 | 9116 |
| 02-Jan-12 | 2000 | 171.301 | 11.67535508 | 4939.164592 | 408000 | 846083.8338 | 438083.8338 | 49.39258965 | 8461 |
| 01-Feb-12 | 2000 | 195.731 | 10.21810546 | 4899.990108 | 410000 | 959079.9638 | 549079.9638 | 49.00092474 | 9591 |
| 01-Mar-12 | 2000 | 201.96 | 9.902951079 | 4860.892134 | 412000 | 981705.7754 | 569705.7754 | 48.60863537 | 9817 |
| 02-Apr-12 | 2000 | 202.455 | 9.878738485 | 4822.162237 | 414000 | 976270.8558 | 562270.8558 | 48.22306191 | 9763 |
| 02-May-12 | 2000 | 198.482 | 10.07648049 | 4784.015656 | 416000 | 949540.9954 | 533540.9954 | 47.83809111 | 9495 |
| 01-Jun-12 | 2000 | 183.658 | 10.88980605 | 4747.067371 | 418000 | 871836.8992 | 453836.8992 | 47.46866458 | 8718 |
| 02-Jul-12 | 2000 | 200.009 | 9.99955002 | 4709.598256 | 420000 | 941962.0377 | 521962.0377 | 47.0978806 | 9420 |
| 01-Aug-12 | 2000 | 197.492 | 10.12699249 | 4672.627368 | 422000 | 922806.5242 | 500806.5242 | 46.72594333 | 9228 |
| 03-Sep-12 | 2000 | 193.362 | 10.34329393 | 4636.244719 | 424000 | 896473.5513 | 472473.5513 | 46.36381502 | 8965 |
| 01-Oct-12 | 2000 | 215.267 | 9.290787719 | 4599.171692 | 426000 | 990049.8925 | 564049.8925 | 45.98939921 | 9900 |
| 01-Nov-12 | 2000 | 211.738 | 9.445635644 | 4562.627928 | 428000 | 966081.7122 | 538081.7122 | 45.62714298 | 9661 |
| 03-Dec-12 | 2000 | 221.297 | 9.037628165 | 4526.038413 | 430000 | 1001598.723 | 571598.7227 | 45.26044185 | 10016 |
| 01-Jan-13 | 2000 | 228.943 | 8.735798867 | 4489.51377 | 432000 | 1027842.751 | 595842.7511 | 44.89327038 | 10278 |
| 01-Feb-13 | 2000 | 230.186 | 8.68862572 | 4453.309126 | 434000 | 1025089.414 | 591089.4144 | 44.53355113 | 10251 |
| 01-Mar-13 | 2000 | 214.304 | 9.332536957 | 4418.108111 | 436000 | 946818.2407 | 510818.2407 | 44.18022995 | 9468 |
| 01-Apr-13 | 2000 | 211.546 | 9.454208541 | 4383.38209 | 438000 | 927286.9476 | 489286.9476 | 43.8344379 | 9273 |

| | | | | | | | | | |
|---|---|---|---|---|---|---|---|---|---|
| 02-May-13 | 2000 | 223.472 | 8.949667072 | 4348.497319 | 440000 | 971767.3929 | 531767.3929 | 43.4864323 | 9718 |
| 03-Jun-13 | 2000 | 219.664 | 9.104814626 | 4314.115701 | 442000 | 947655.9114 | 505655.9114 | 43.14316411 | 9477 |
| 01-Jul-13 | 2000 | 213.882 | 9.350950524 | 4280.323488 | 444000 | 915484.1482 | 471484.1482 | 42.80397602 | 9155 |
| 01-Aug-13 | 2000 | 198.97 | 10.0517666 | 4247.571278 | 446000 | 845139.2573 | 399139.2573 | 42.47373976 | 8451 |
| 02-Sep-13 | 2000 | 195.575 | 10.22625591 | 4215.323795 | 448000 | 824411.9511 | 376411.9511 | 42.15262687 | 8244 |
| 01-Oct-13 | 2000 | 203.838 | 9.811713223 | 4182.982881 | 450000 | 852650.8645 | 402650.8645 | 41.83223933 | 8527 |
| 01-Nov-13 | 2000 | 228.138 | 8.76662371 | 4149.917265 | 452000 | 946753.8251 | 494753.8251 | 41.50119664 | 9468 |
| 02-Dec-13 | 2000 | 228.694 | 8.745310327 | 4117.161379 | 454000 | 941570.1044 | 487570.1044 | 41.17292102 | 9416 |
| 01-Jan-14 | 2000 | 235.415 | 8.495635367 | 4084.484093 | 456000 | 961548.8228 | 505548.8228 | 40.84276703 | 9615 |
| 03-Feb-14 | 2000 | 219.941 | 9.093347761 | 4052.734674 | 458000 | 891362.517 | 433362.517 | 40.52905097 | 8914 |
| 03-Mar-14 | 2000 | 229.238 | 8.724557011 | 4020.93018 | 460000 | 921749.9926 | 461749.9926 | 40.20712098 | 9217 |
| 01-Apr-14 | 2000 | 254.063 | 7.872063228 | 3988.595122 | 462000 | 1013354.443 | 551354.4426 | 39.88774438 | 10134 |
| 02-May-14 | 2000 | 257.035 | 7.781041492 | 3956.488419 | 464000 | 1016956.001 | 552956.0009 | 39.56659599 | 10170 |
| 02-Jun-14 | 2000 | 300.302 | 6.659962305 | 3923.581786 | 466000 | 1178259.457 | 712259.4574 | 39.23716792 | 11783 |
| 01-Jul-14 | 2000 | 314.828 | 6.352675111 | 3890.697293 | 468000 | 1224900.447 | 756900.4474 | 38.90695872 | 12249 |
| 01-Aug-14 | 2000 | 306.05 | 6.534879922 | 3858.325214 | 470000 | 1180840.432 | 710840.4318 | 38.58193106 | 11808 |
| 01-Sep-14 | 2000 | 327.618 | 6.104670684 | 3825.847954 | 472000 | 1253416.655 | 781416.6549 | 38.25797117 | 12534 |
| 01-Oct-14 | 2000 | 322.203 | 6.207266847 | 3793.79725 | 474000 | 1222372.855 | 748372.8552 | 37.93881497 | 12224 |
| 03-Nov-14 | 2000 | 341.598 | 5.854835216 | 3761.71327 | 476000 | 1284993.73 | 808993.7295 | 37.61731626 | 12850 |
| 01-Dec-14 | 2000 | 354.292 | 5.645061136 | 3729.741015 | 478000 | 1321417.404 | 843417.4036 | 37.29691893 | 13214 |
| 01-Jan-15 | 2000 | 345.351 | 5.791209523 | 3698.235305 | 480000 | 1277189.261 | 797189.2609 | 36.98266401 | 12772 |
| 02-Feb-15 | 2000 | 359.808 | 5.5585201 | 3666.811161 | 482000 | 1319347.99 | 837347.9903 | 36.66677784 | 13193 |
| 02-Mar-15 | 2000 | 361.473 | 5.532916705 | 3635.6773 | 484000 | 1314199.181 | 830199.1807 | 36.35679567 | 13142 |
| 01-Apr-15 | 2000 | 346.246 | 5.776240014 | 3605.096745 | 486000 | 1248250.327 | 762250.3274 | 36.05240205 | 12483 |
| 04-May-15 | 2000 | 340.055 | 5.881401538 | 3574.925744 | 488000 | 1215671.374 | 727671.3739 | 35.75009925 | 12157 |
| 01-Jun-15 | 2000 | 342.512 | 5.839211473 | 3545.014856 | 490000 | 1214210.128 | 724210.1284 | 35.44985285 | 12142 |
| 01-Jul-15 | 2000 | 341.717 | 5.85279632 | 3515.4178 | 492000 | 1201278.024 | 709278.0243 | 35.15482109 | 12013 |
| 03-Aug-15 | 2000 | 352.187 | 5.678801319 | 3485.94178 | 494000 | 1227703.378 | 733703.3776 | 34.85932189 | 12277 |
| 01-Sep-15 | 2000 | 317.114 | 6.306880176 | 3457.389338 | 496000 | 1096386.563 | 600386.5626 | 34.57431712 | 10964 |
| 01-Oct-15 | 2000 | 322.533 | 6.200915875 | 3429.015937 | 498000 | 1105970.797 | 607970.7972 | 34.29106479 | 11060 |
| 02-Nov-15 | 2000 | 328.504 | 6.088205927 | 3400.813078 | 500000 | 1117180.699 | 617180.6994 | 34.00871831 | 11172 |
| 01-Dec-15 | 2000 | 330.806 | 6.045839556 | 3372.850199 | 502000 | 1115759.083 | 613759.083 | 33.72973888 | 11158 |
| 01-Jan-16 | 2000 | 326.019 | 6.134611786 | 3345.255072 | 504000 | 1090616.713 | 586616.7134 | 33.45203807 | 10906 |
| 01-Feb-16 | 2000 | 296.937 | 6.735435463 | 3318.53847 | 506000 | 985396.8576 | 479396.8576 | 33.18549052 | 9854 |
| 01-Mar-16 | 2000 | 279.887 | 7.14574096 | 3292.49872 | 508000 | 921527.5893 | 413527.5893 | 32.92400147 | 9215 |
| **toatal** | **508000** | | | | | | | | **1398879** |

# 4

# A Lump Sum Investment vs SIP

I know that among my readers, there may be mathematicians, engineers and people with sharp mathematical minds. After reading the previous chapter, a question must have arisen in their minds– can a lump sum investment instead of SIP generate regular income from Systematic Withdrawal Plan?

In the previous chapter, I explained how in April 1999 an initial investment of ₹ 1 lakh in a mutual fund was made and then a SIP of ₹ 2,000 per month for 17 years was continued. After one year, to get 1% amount of the total fund value per month, we were getting 1% monthly income of the fund value every month by selling so many units.

This method was so successful that we booked a tax-free profit of ₹ 13,98,879 by making a total investment of 5,08,000 in 17 years. Even after that, we had a profit balance of 4,13,527 in our holding and after 17 years, a monthly tax-free profit of ₹ 10,000 income was being received.

I told you in the previous chapter that you should undertake an SIP equal to 2% of the lump sum investment and keep withdrawing 1% of the fund value every month by selling it. That is, if you have invested 1,00,000 as a lump sum, then the SIP of 2% of its amount has to be continued ie, 2,000 per month. Receivable units have to be sold every month at 1% of the total fund value generated.

Now the learned readers will wonder what is the use of buying new units every month, while selling some old ones? Why should we bother so much? It is better if you keep selling units of only 1% of the fund value every month and you can receive a regular income.

Another question may also come to your mind – if we had made a lump sum investment of onc lakh in 1999 and after 1 year, we had kept on withdrawing 1% of the fund value by selling units, would we have got a regular monthly income? If yes, for how long and for how much?

So, let's find the answers. At the outset, a self-evident fact requires no proof. We will re-use the data from 1st April, 1999 to 1st March, 2016 of HDFC Top 200 Fund G Plans given in the previous chapter. This time, we'll not keep a monthly SIP. In a very simple way, after 1 year of investment of 1 lakh (when the unit will become tax free according to long term capital gains) we will sell that many units per month so that we get a monthly income equal to 1% of some fund value.

The complete details are given in Appendix 'D' at the end of the book. You can see its calculation sheet there.

You'll see that even in this method, there would have been a regular income per month for 17 consecutive years, which would have started from ₹ 1,540 per month. This would increase to 3,000 to 4,000 per month by the end. And on a total investment of 1 lakh, you would get tax free profit of ₹ 5,42,931 as regular monthly income. After 17 years, as on 1st March, 2016 the value of your remaining units would also have been ₹ 3,03,171 which could have given you regular monthly income for almost 3 years in the future. So, overall, the conclusion is that the lump sum investment and 2% monthly SIP method of investment is better than a lump sum investment method because in this (in lump sum investment) by selling units every month, the number of units keeps decreasing continuously and in about 20 years, the whole unit is exhausted.

The monthly income also does not increase continuously, whereas the monthly income in the SIP method with lump sum investment went up to ₹ 10,000 per month.

Therefore, it is better to choose a lump sum investment and a monthly SIP equal to 2% of the lump sum investment. Decide on the amount which will always be constant. But we will book monthly income equal to 1% of the fund value by reviewing the fund value every month. This will not reduce the number of units, and this system will be able to produce a regular accelerating monthly income for 30-40 years.

## Summary

1. Investing in mutual funds is subject to market risk. Hence, it does not guarantee regular monthly income like bank interest.

2. My combination of lump sum investment with SIP is more effective as compared to getting a monthly income by investing a lump sum and then selling units.

❑

# APPENDIX-D

| Investment Date | Investment | NAV | Units Purchased | total units in folio | total investment at cost | total fund value at NAV | net profit/loss | Redumption | monthly income |
|---|---|---|---|---|---|---|---|---|---|
| 01-Mar-99 | 1,00,000 | 13.54 | 7385.524372 | 7385.524372 | 100000 | 100000 | 0 | | 0 |
| 01-Apr-99 | | 14.49 | 0 | 7385.524372 | 100000 | 107016.2482 | 7016.248154 | 0 | 0 |
| 03-May-99 | | 13.36 | 0 | 7385.524372 | 100000 | 98670.60561 | -1329.394387 | 0 | 0 |
| 01-Jun-99 | | 14.42 | 0 | 7385.524372 | 100000 | 106499.2614 | 6499.261448 | 0 | 0 |
| 01-Jul-99 | | 14.43 | 0 | 7385.524372 | 100000 | 106573.1167 | 6573.116691 | 0 | 0 |
| 02-Aug-99 | | 16.51 | 0 | 7385.524372 | 100000 | 121935.0074 | 21935.00739 | 0 | 0 |
| 01-Sep-99 | | 18.39 | 0 | 7385.524372 | 100000 | 135819.7932 | 35819.79321 | 0 | 0 |
| 01-Oct-99 | | 18.94 | 0 | 7385.524372 | 100000 | 139881.8316 | 39881.83161 | 0 | 0 |
| 01-Nov-99 | | 16.32 | 0 | 7385.524372 | 100000 | 120531.7578 | 20531.75775 | 0 | 0 |
| 01-Dec-99 | | 18.4 | 0 | 7385.524372 | 100000 | 135893.6484 | 35893.64845 | 0 | 0 |
| 03-Jan-00 | | 21.68 | 0 | 7385.524372 | 100000 | 160118.1684 | 60118.16839 | 0 | 0 |
| 01-Feb-00 | | 22.11 | 0 | 7385.524372 | 100000 | 163293.9439 | 63293.94387 | 0 | 0 |
| 01-Mar-00 | | 24.32 | 0 | 7385.524372 | 100000 | 179615.9527 | 79615.95273 | 0 | 0 |
| 03-Apr-00 | | 20.85 | 0 | 7385.524372 | 100000 | 153988.1832 | 53988.18316 | 73.86091127 | 1540 |
| 02-May-00 | | 15.7 | 0 | 7311.663461 | 100000 | 114793.1163 | 14793.11634 | 73.12101911 | 1148 |
| 01-Jun-00 | | 15.7 | 0 | 7238.542442 | 100000 | 113645.1163 | 13645.11634 | 72.3566879 | 1136 |
| 03-Jul-00 | | 17.4 | 0 | 7166.185754 | 100000 | 124691.6321 | 24691.63212 | 71.66666667 | 1247 |
| 01-Aug-00 | | 15.33 | 0 | 7094.519087 | 100000 | 108758.9776 | 8758.977608 | 70.97195042 | 1088 |
| 04-Sep-00 | | 16.7 | 0 | 7023.547137 | 100000 | 117293.2372 | 17293.23719 | 70.23952096 | 1173 |
| 03-Oct-00 | | 14.28 | 0 | 6953.307616 | 100000 | 99293.23276 | -706.7672449 | 69.53781513 | 993 |
| 01-Nov-00 | | 13.93 | 0 | 6883.769801 | 100000 | 95890.91332 | -4109.086675 | 68.84422111 | 959 |
| 01-Dec-00 | | 14.98 | 0 | 6814.92558 | 100000 | 102087.5852 | 2087.585183 | 68.15754339 | 1021 |
| 01-Jan-01 | | 15.26 | 0 | 6746.768036 | 100000 | 102955.6802 | 2955.680234 | 67.49672346 | 1030 |
| 01-Feb-01 | | 15.67 | 0 | 6679.271313 | 100000 | 104664.1815 | 4664.181472 | 66.81557116 | 1047 |
| 01-Mar-01 | | 16.12 | 0 | 6612.455742 | 100000 | 106592.7866 | 6592.786556 | 66.12903226 | 1066 |
| 02-Apr-01 | | 13.28 | 0 | 6546.326709 | 100000 | 86935.2187 | -13064.7813 | 65.43674699 | 869 |
| 02-May-01 | | 14.19 | 0 | 6480.889962 | 100000 | 91963.82857 | -8036.171433 | 64.83439042 | 920 |
| 01-Jun-01 | | 14.34 | 0 | 6416.055572 | 100000 | 92006.2369 | -7993.763097 | 64.15620642 | 920 |
| 02-Jul-01 | | 13.57 | 0 | 6351.899366 | 100000 | 86195.27439 | -13804.72561 | 63.52247605 | 862 |
| 01-Aug-01 | | 13.16 | 0 | 6288.37689 | 100000 | 82755.03987 | -17244.96013 | 62.91793313 | 828 |
| 03-Sep-01 | | 13.15 | 0 | 6225.458956 | 100000 | 81864.78528 | -18135.21472 | 62.28136882 | 819 |
| 01-Oct-01 | | 11.71 | 0 | 6163.177588 | 100000 | 72170.80955 | -27829.19045 | 61.65670367 | 722 |

| | | | | | | | |
|---|---|---|---|---|---|---|---|
| 01-Nov-01 | 12.88 | 0 | 6101.520884 | 100000 | 78587.58898 | -21412.41102 | 61.02484472 | 786 |
| 03-Dec-01 | 13.8 | 0 | 6040.496039 | 100000 | 83358.84534 | -16641.15466 | 60.43478261 | 834 |
| 01-Jan-02 | 13.57 | 0 | 5980.061257 | 100000 | 81149.43125 | -18850.56875 | 59.7641857 | 811 |
| 01-Feb-02 | 14.73 | 0 | 5920.297071 | 100000 | 87205.97585 | -12794.02415 | 59.19891378 | 872 |
| 01-Mar-02 | 16.48 | 0 | 5861.098157 | 100000 | 96590.89763 | -3409.102371 | 58.61650485 | 966 |
| 01-Apr-02 | 16.93 | 0 | 5802.481652 | 100000 | 98236.01437 | -1763.985627 | 58.003544 | 982 |
| 02-May-02 | 16.9 | 0 | 5744.478108 | 100000 | 97081.68003 | -2918.319971 | 57.4556213 | 971 |
| 03-Jun-02 | 15.9 | 0 | 5687.022487 | 100000 | 90423.65754 | -9576.342458 | 56.85534591 | 904 |
| 01-Jul-02 | 16.5 | 0 | 5630.167141 | 100000 | 92897.75783 | -7102.242173 | 56.3030303 | 929 |
| 01-Aug-02 | 15.55 | 0 | 5573.864111 | 100000 | 86673.58692 | -13326.41308 | 55.75562701 | 867 |
| 02-Sep-02 | 16.37 | 0 | 5518.108484 | 100000 | 90331.43588 | -9668.564122 | 55.16188149 | 903 |
| 01-Oct-02 | 14.9 | 0 | 5462.946602 | 100000 | 81397.90437 | -18602.09563 | 54.63087248 | 814 |
| 01-Nov-02 | 15.29 | 0 | 5408.31573 | 100000 | 82693.14751 | -17306.85249 | 54.08763898 | 827 |
| 02-Dec-02 | 16.57 | 0 | 5354.228091 | 100000 | 88719.55946 | -11280.44054 | 53.53047677 | 887 |
| 01-Jan-03 | 17.36 | 0 | 5300.697614 | 100000 | 92020.11058 | -7979.889421 | 52.99539171 | 920 |
| 03-Feb-03 | 17.34 | 0 | 5247.702222 | 100000 | 90995.15653 | -9004.843465 | 52.47981546 | 910 |
| 03-Mar-03 | 17.58 | 0 | 5195.222407 | 100000 | 91332.00991 | -8667.990088 | 51.93401593 | 913 |
| 01-Apr-03 | 16.71 | 0 | 5143.288391 | 100000 | 85944.34901 | -14055.65099 | 51.40634351 | 859 |
| 02-May-03 | 17.64 | 0 | 5091.882047 | 100000 | 89820.79932 | -10179.20068 | 50.90702948 | 898 |
| 02-Jun-03 | 20.84 | 0 | 5040.975018 | 100000 | 105053.9194 | 5053.919374 | 50.4318618 | 1051 |
| 01-Jul-03 | 23.057 | 0 | 4990.543156 | 100000 | 115066.9536 | 15066.95355 | 49.91976406 | 1151 |
| 01-Aug-03 | 24.408 | 0 | 4940.623392 | 100000 | 120590.7358 | 20590.73575 | 49.4100295 | 1206 |
| 01-Sep-03 | 29.168 | 0 | 4891.213363 | 100000 | 142666.9114 | 42666.91136 | 48.92347778 | 1427 |
| 01-Oct-03 | 30.215 | 0 | 4842.289885 | 100000 | 146309.7889 | 46309.78887 | 48.41965911 | 1463 |
| 03-Nov-03 | 33.876 | 0 | 4793.870226 | 100000 | 162397.1478 | 62397.14776 | 47.93954422 | 1624 |
| 01-Dec-03 | 35.192 | 0 | 4745.930681 | 100000 | 167018.7925 | 67018.79254 | 47.45396681 | 1670 |
| 01-Jan-04 | 41.043 | 0 | 4698.476715 | 100000 | 192839.5798 | 92839.5798 | 46.97512365 | 1928 |
| 03-Feb-04 | 38.825 | 0 | 4651.501591 | 100000 | 180594.5493 | 80594.54927 | 46.51641983 | 1806 |
| 01-Mar-04 | 40.865 | 0 | 4604.985171 | 100000 | 188182.719 | 88182.71902 | 46.05408051 | 1882 |
| 01-Apr-04 | 41.106 | 0 | 4558.931091 | 100000 | 187399.4214 | 87399.42141 | 45.58945166 | 1874 |
| 03-May-04 | 41.075 | 0 | 4513.341639 | 100000 | 185385.5078 | 85385.50782 | 45.13694461 | 1854 |
| 01-Jun-04 | 35.633 | 0 | 4468.204694 | 100000 | 159215.5379 | 59215.53787 | 44.67768641 | 1592 |
| 01-Jul-04 | 36.701 | 0 | 4423.527008 | 100000 | 162347.8647 | 62347.86472 | 44.22222828 | 1623 |
| 02-Aug-04 | 38.849 | 0 | 4379.30478 | 100000 | 170131.6114 | 70131.61139 | 43.78491081 | 1701 |
| 01-Sep-04 | 40.019 | 0 | 4335.519869 | 100000 | 173503.1696 | 73503.16963 | 43.35440666 | 1735 |

| | | | | | | | | |
|---|---|---|---|---|---|---|---|---|
| 01-Oct-04 | 42.931 | 0 | 4292.165462 | 100000 | 184266.9555 | 84266.95546 | 42.92935175 | 1843 |
| 01-Nov-04 | 43.397 | 0 | 4249.23611 | 100000 | 184404.0995 | 84404.09949 | 42.49141646 | 1844 |
| 01-Dec-04 | 47.125 | 0 | 4206.744694 | 100000 | 198242.8437 | 98242.8437 | 42.05835544 | 1982 |
| 03-Jan-05 | 52.294 | 0 | 4164.686339 | 100000 | 217788.1074 | 117788.1074 | 41.64913757 | 2178 |
| 01-Feb-05 | 50.394 | 0 | 4123.037201 | 100000 | 207776.3367 | 107776.3367 | 41.23506767 | 2078 |
| 01-Mar-05 | 52.786 | 0 | 4081.802133 | 100000 | 215462.0074 | 115462.0074 | 40.82521881 | 2155 |
| 01-Apr-05 | 53.222 | 0 | 4040.976915 | 100000 | 215068.8733 | 115068.8733 | 40.4156176 | 2151 |
| 02-May-05 | 50.255 | 0 | 4000.561297 | 100000 | 201048.208 | 101048.208 | 39.9960203 | 2010 |
| 01-Jun-05 | 54.973 | 0 | 3960.565277 | 100000 | 217724.155 | 117724.155 | 39.6012588 | 2177 |
| 01-Jul-05 | 57.492 | 0 | 3920.964018 | 100000 | 225424.0633 | 125424.0633 | 39.20545467 | 2254 |
| 01-Aug-05 | 60.918 | 0 | 3881.758563 | 100000 | 236468.9681 | 136468.9681 | 38.82267967 | 2365 |
| 01-Sep-05 | 64.253 | 0 | 3842.935883 | 100000 | 246920.1593 | 146920.1593 | 38.42622134 | 2469 |
| 03-Oct-05 | 70.553 | 0 | 3804.509662 | 100000 | 268419.5702 | 168419.5702 | 38.04232279 | 2684 |
| 02-Nov-05 | 66.878 | 0 | 3766.467339 | 100000 | 251893.8027 | 151893.8027 | 37.66560005 | 2519 |
| 01-Dec-05 | 75.162 | 0 | 3728.801739 | 100000 | 280264.1963 | 180264.1963 | 37.29278093 | 2803 |
| 02-Jan-06 | 79.874 | 0 | 3691.508958 | 100000 | 294855.5865 | 194855.5865 | 36.92065002 | 2949 |
| 01-Feb-06 | 84.001 | 0 | 3654.588308 | 100000 | 306989.0725 | 206989.0725 | 36.54718396 | 3070 |
| 01-Mar-06 | 89.277 | 0 | 3618.041124 | 100000 | 323007.8575 | 223007.8575 | 36.17953112 | 3230 |
| 03-Apr-06 | 98.486 | 0 | 3581.861593 | 100000 | 352763.2209 | 252763.2209 | 35.82235038 | 3528 |
| 02-May-06 | 101.43 | 0 | 3546.039243 | 100000 | 359674.7604 | 259674.7604 | 35.4628808 | 3597 |
| 01-Jun-06 | 84.905 | 0 | 3510.576362 | 100000 | 298065.486 | 198065.486 | 35.10982863 | 2981 |
| 03-Jul-06 | 86.3 | 0 | 3475.466533 | 100000 | 299932.7618 | 199932.7618 | 34.75086906 | 2999 |
| 01-Aug-06 | 87.295 | 0 | 3440.715664 | 100000 | 300357.2739 | 200357.2739 | 34.41205109 | 3004 |
| 01-Sep-06 | 96.306 | 0 | 3406.303613 | 100000 | 328047.4758 | 228047.4758 | 34.05810645 | 3280 |
| 03-Oct-06 | 100.218 | 0 | 3372.245507 | 100000 | 337959.7002 | 237959.7002 | 33.72647628 | 3380 |
| 01-Nov-06 | 105.66 | 0 | 3338.519031 | 100000 | 352747.9208 | 252747.9208 | 33.38065493 | 3527 |
| 01-Dec-06 | 110.994 | 0 | 3305.138376 | 100000 | 366850.5289 | 266850.5289 | 33.05584086 | 3669 |
| 02-Jan-07 | 110.855 | 0 | 3272.082535 | 100000 | 362726.7094 | 262726.7094 | 32.71841595 | 3627 |
| 01-Feb-07 | 113.266 | 0 | 3239.364119 | 100000 | 366909.8163 | 266909.8163 | 32.39277453 | 3669 |
| 01-Mar-07 | 104.794 | 0 | 3206.971344 | 100000 | 336071.3551 | 236071.3551 | 32.0724469 | 3361 |
| 02-Apr-07 | 100.009 | 0 | 3174.898897 | 100000 | 317518.4638 | 217518.4638 | 31.74714276 | 3175 |
| 03-May-07 | 113.528 | 0 | 3143.151755 | 100000 | 356835.7324 | 256835.7324 | 31.42837009 | 3568 |
| 01-Jun-07 | 119.524 | 0 | 3111.723385 | 100000 | 371925.6258 | 271925.6258 | 31.11508986 | 3719 |
| 02-Jul-07 | 121.292 | 0 | 3080.608295 | 100000 | 373653.1413 | 273653.1413 | 30.80994625 | 3737 |
| 01-Aug-07 | 122.866 | 0 | 3049.798348 | 100000 | 374716.5239 | 274716.5239 | 30.49663861 | 3747 |

| | | | | | | | | |
|---|---|---|---|---|---|---|---|---|
| 03-Sep-07 | 127.093 | 0 | 3019.30171 | 100000 | 383732.1122 | 283732.1122 | 30.19049043 | 3837 |
| 01-Oct-07 | 141.248 | 0 | 2989.111219 | 100000 | 422205.9815 | 322205.9815 | 29.89068872 | 4222 |
| 01-Nov-07 | 159.7 | 0 | 2959.220531 | 100000 | 472587.5187 | 372587.5187 | 29.59298685 | 4726 |
| 03-Dec-07 | 160.418 | 0 | 2929.627544 | 100000 | 469964.9913 | 369964.9913 | 29.29845778 | 4700 |
| 01-Jan-08 | 170.241 | 0 | 2900.329086 | 100000 | 493754.9239 | 393754.9239 | 29.00593864 | 4938 |
| 01-Feb-08 | 151.276 | 0 | 2871.323147 | 100000 | 434362.2804 | 334362.2804 | 28.7157249 | 4344 |
| 03-Mar-08 | 141.867 | 0 | 2842.607423 | 100000 | 403272.1872 | 303272.1872 | 28.42803471 | 4033 |
| 01-Apr-08 | 130.829 | 0 | 2814.179388 | 100000 | 368176.2751 | 268176.2751 | 28.1436073 | 3682 |
| 02-May-08 | 145.16 | 0 | 2786.03578 | 100000 | 404420.9539 | 304420.9539 | 27.8589143 | 4044 |
| 02-Jun-08 | 135.425 | 0 | 2758.176866 | 100000 | 373526.1021 | 273526.1021 | 27.57984124 | 3735 |
| 01-Jul-08 | 111.825 | 0 | 2730.597025 | 100000 | 305349.0123 | 205349.0123 | 27.3015873 | 3053 |
| 01-Aug-08 | 126.743 | 0 | 2703.295438 | 100000 | 342623.7737 | 242623.7737 | 27.03107864 | 3426 |
| 01-Sep-08 | 129.16 | 0 | 2676.264359 | 100000 | 345666.3046 | 245666.3046 | 26.7652524 | 3457 |
| 01-Oct-08 | 120.227 | 0 | 2649.499107 | 100000 | 318541.3291 | 218541.3291 | 26.49155348 | 3185 |
| 03-Nov-08 | 95.928 | 0 | 2623.007553 | 100000 | 251619.8686 | 151619.8686 | 26.22800434 | 2516 |
| 01-Dec-08 | 84.587 | 0 | 2596.779549 | 100000 | 219653.7917 | 119653.7917 | 25.9732583 | 2197 |
| 01-Jan-09 | 94.479 | 0 | 2570.80629 | 100000 | 242887.2075 | 142887.2075 | 25.70941691 | 2429 |
| 02-Feb-09 | 85.752 | 0 | 2545.096874 | 100000 | 218247.1471. | 118247.1471 | 25.44547066 | 2182 |
| 02-Mar-09 | 82.213 | 0 | 2519.651403 | 100000 | 207148.1008 | 107148.1008 | 25.19066328 | 2071 |
| 01-Apr-09 | 93.541 | 0 | 2494.46074 | 100000 | 233334.352 | 133334.352 | 24.94093499 | 2333 |
| 04-May-09 | 113.162 | 0 | 2469.519805 | 100000 | 279455.8001 | 179455.8001 | 24.69910394 | 2795 |
| 01-Jun-09 | 140.372 | 0 | 2444.820701 | 100000 | 343184.3714 | 243184.3714 | 24.44932038 | 3432 |
| 01-Jul-09 | 145.276 | 0 | 2420.37138 | 100000 | 351621.8727 | 251621.8727 | 24.20220821 | 3516 |
| 03-Aug-09 | 158.221 | 0 | 2396.169172 | 100000 | 379124.2826 | 279124.2826 | 23.960157 | 3791 |
| 01-Sep-09 | 157.155 | 0 | 2372.209015 | 100000 | 372804.5078 | 272804.5078 | 23.72180332 | 3728 |
| 01-Oct-09 | 171.852 | 0 | 2348.487212 | 100000 | 403592.2243 | 303592.2243 | 23.48532458 | 4036 |
| 03-Nov-09 | 162.803 | 0 | 2325.001887 | 100000 | 378517.2822 | 278517.2822 | 23.24895733 | 3785 |
| 01-Dec-09 | 178.983 | 0 | 2301.75293 | 100000 | 411974.6447 | 311974.6447 | 23.01894593 | 4120 |
| 04-Jan-10 | 181.428 | 0 | 2278.733984 | 100000 | 413426.1492 | 313426.1492 | 22.78589854 | 4134 |
| 01-Feb-10 | 173.925 | 0 | 2255.948085 | 100000 | 392365.7708 | 292365.7708 | 22.5614489 | 3924 |
| 02-Mar-10 | 176.554 | 0 | 2233.386637 | 100000 | 394313.3442 | 294313.3442 | 22.33311055 | 3943 |
| 01-Apr-10 | 184.923 | 0 | 2211.053526 | 100000 | 408874.6512 | 308874.6512 | 22.11190604 | 4089 |
| 03-May-10 | 186.819 | 0 | 2188.94162 | 100000 | 408935.8845 | 308935.8845 | 21.88749538 | 4089 |
| 01-Jun-10 | 181.953 | 0 | 2167.054125 | 100000 | 394301.9991 | 294301.9991 | 21.67043138 | 3943 |
| 01-Jul-10 | 192.971 | 0 | 2145.383693 | 100000 | 413996.8367 | 313996.8367 | 21.45400086 | 4140 |

| | | | | | | | | |
|---|---|---|---|---|---|---|---|---|
| 02-Aug-10 | 201.717 | 0 | 2123.929692 | 100000 | 428432.7257 | 328432.7257 | 21.23767456 | 4284 |
| 01-Sep-10 | 207.327 | 0 | 2102.692018 | 100000 | 435944.828 | 335944.828 | 21.02475799 | 4359 |
| 01-Oct-10 | 227.948 | 0 | 2081.66726 | 100000 | 474511.8885 | 374511.8885 | 20.81615105 | 4745 |
| 01-Nov-10 | 229.976 | 0 | 2060.851109 | 100000 | 473946.2946 | 373946.2946 | 20.60649807 | 4739 |
| 01-Dec-10 | 226.017 | 0 | 2040.244611 | 100000 | 461129.9662 | 361129.9662 | 20.40112027 | 4611 |
| 03-Jan-11 | 226.586 | 0 | 2019.84349 | 100000 | 457668.2571 | 357668.2571 | 20.19983582 | 4577 |
| 01-Feb-11 | 202.436 | 0 | 1999.643655 | 100000 | 404799.8629 | 304799.8629 | 19.99644332 | 4048 |
| 01-Mar-11 | 204.031 | 0 | 1979.647211 | 100000 | 403909.4002 | 303909.4002 | 19.79601139 | 4039 |
| 01-Apr-11 | 214.836 | 0 | 1959.8512 | 100000 | 421046.5924 | 321046.5924 | 19.59634326 | 4210 |
| 02-May-11 | 213.073 | 0 | 1940.254857 | 100000 | 413415.9231 | 313415.9231 | 19.40180126 | 4134 |
| 01-Jun-11 | 210.437 | 0 | 1920.853055 | 100000 | 404218.5544 | 304218.5544 | 19.20764885 | 4042 |
| 01-Jul-11 | 211.831 | 0 | 1901.645406 | 100000 | 402827.4481 | 302827.4481 | 19.01515831 | 4028 |
| 01-Aug-11 | 208.824 | 0 | 1882.630248 | 100000 | 393138.3789 | 293138.3789 | 18.82446462 | 3931 |
| 02-Sep-11 | 190.774 | 0 | 1863.805784 | 100000 | 355565.6846 | 255565.6846 | 18.63985658 | 3556 |
| 03-Oct-11 | 184.462 | 0 | 1845.165927 | 100000 | 340362.9972 | 240362.9972 | 18.45366525 | 3404 |
| 01-Nov-11 | 195.68 | 0 | 1826.712262 | 100000 | 357451.0554 | 257451.0554 | 18.26962388 | 3575 |
| 01-Dec-11 | 183.153 | 0 | 1808.442638 | 100000 | 331221.6944 | 231221.6944 | 18.08324188 | 3312 |
| 02-Jan-12 | 171.301 | 0 | 1790.359396 | 100000 | 306690.3549 | 206690.3549 | 17.90415701 | 3067 |
| 01-Feb-12 | 195.731 | 0 | 1772.455239 | 100000 | 346924.4364 | 246924.4364 | 17.72330392 | 3469 |
| 01-Mar-12 | 201.96 | 0 | 1754.731935 | 100000 | 354385.6616 | 254385.6616 | 17.54802931 | 3544 |
| 02-Apr-12 | 202.455 | 0 | 1737.183906 | 100000 | 351701.5676 | 251701.5676 | 17.37176163 | 3517 |
| 02-May-12 | 198.482 | 0 | 1719.812144 | 100000 | 341351.754 | 241351.754 | 17.20055219 | 3414 |
| 01-Jun-12 | 183.658 | 0 | 1702.611592 | 100000 | 312698.2397 | 212698.2397 | 17.02621176 | 3127 |
| 02-Jul-12 | 200.009 | 0 | 1685.58538 | 100000 | 337132.2463 | 237132.2463 | 16.85424156 | 3371 |
| 01-Aug-12 | 197.492 | 0 | 1668.731139 | 100000 | 329561.05 | 229561.05 | 16.68928362 | 3296 |
| 03-Sep-12 | 193.362 | 0 | 1652.041855 | 100000 | 319442.1172 | 219442.1172 | 16.5182404 | 3194 |
| 01-Oct-12 | 215.267 | 0 | 1635.523615 | 100000 | 352074.2619 | 252074.2619 | 16.35643178 | 3521 |
| 01-Nov-12 | 211.738 | 0 | 1619.167183 | 100000 | 342839.2209 | 242839.2209 | 16.18981949 | 3428 |
| 03-Dec-12 | 221.297 | 0 | 1602.977363 | 100000 | 354734.0816 | 254734.0816 | 16.02823355 | 3547 |
| 01-Jan-13 | 228.943 | 0 | 1586.94913 | 100000 | 363320.8946 | 263320.8946 | 15.86857864 | 3633 |
| 01-Feb-13 | 230.186 | 0 | 1571.080551 | 100000 | 361640.7477 | 261640.7477 | 15.7090353 | 3616 |
| 01-Mar-13 | 214.304 | 0 | 1555.371516 | 100000 | 333322.3373 | 233322.3373 | 15.55267284 | 3333 |
| 01-Apr-13 | 211.546 | 0 | 1539.818843 | 100000 | 325742.517 | 225742.517 | 15.39617861 | 3257 |
| 02-May-13 | 223.472 | 0 | 1524.422664 | 100000 | 340665.7816 | 240665.7816 | 15.24575786 | 3407 |
| 03-Jun-13 | 219.664 | 0 | 1509.176906 | 100000 | 331511.836 | 231511.836 | 15.09123024 | 3315 |

| | | | | | | | | | |
|---|---|---|---|---|---|---|---|---|---|
| 01-Jul-13 | | 213.882 | 0 | 1494.085676 | 100000 | 319558.0326 | 219558.0326 | 14.94281894 | 3196 |
| 01-Aug-13 | | 198.97 | 0 | 1479.142857 | 100000 | 294305.0543 | 194305.0543 | 14.79117455 | 2943 |
| 02-Sep-13 | | 195.575 | 0 | 1464.351683 | 100000 | 286390.5804 | 186390.5804 | 14.64399847 | 2864 |
| 01-Oct-13 | | 203.838 | 0 | 1449.707684 | 100000 | 295505.515 | 195505.515 | 14.49680629 | 2955 |
| 01-Nov-13 | | 228.138 | 0 | 1435.210878 | 100000 | 327426.1393 | 227426.1393 | 14.35096301 | 3274 |
| 02-Dec-13 | | 228.694 | 0 | 1420.859915 | 100000 | 324942.1374 | 224942.1374 | 14.20675663 | 3249 |
| 01-Jan-14 | | 235.415 | 0 | 1406.653158 | 100000 | 331147.2533 | 231147.2533 | 14.06452435 | 3311 |
| 03-Feb-14 | | 219.941 | 0 | 1392.588634 | 100000 | 306287.3368 | 206287.3368 | 13.9264621 | 3063 |
| 03-Mar-14 | | 229.238 | 0 | 1378.662172 | 100000 | 316041.759 | 216041.759 | 13.78480008 | 3160 |
| 01-Apr-14 | | 254.063 | 0 | 1364.877372 | 100000 | 346764.8397 | 246764.8397 | 13.65015764 | 3468 |
| 02-May-14 | | 257.035 | 0 | 1351.227214 | 100000 | 347312.687 | 247312.687 | 13.51177855 | 3473 |
| 02-Jun-14 | | 300.302 | 0 | 1337.715436 | 100000 | 401718.6208 | 301718.6208 | 13.37653429 | 4017 |
| 01-Jul-14 | | 314.828 | 0 | 1324.338901 | 100000 | 416938.9676 | 316938.9676 | 13.24215127 | 4169 |
| 01-Aug-14 | | 306.05 | 0 | 1311.09675 | 100000 | 401261.1604 | 301261.1604 | 13.11223656 | 4013 |
| 01-Sep-14 | | 327.618 | 0 | 1297.984514 | 100000 | 425243.0904 | 325243.0904 | 12.97852987 | 4252 |
| 01-Oct-14 | | 322.203 | 0 | 1285.005984 | 100000 | 414032.783 | 314032.783 | 12.84904237 | 4140 |
| 03-Nov-14 | | 341.598 | 0 | 1272.156941 | 100000 | 434566.2668 | 334566.2668 | 12.72255692 | 4346 |
| 01-Dec-14 | | 354.292 | 0 | 1259.434384 | 100000 | 446207.5269 | 346207.5269 | 12.59413139 | 4462 |
| 01-Jan-15 | | 345.351 | 0 | 1246.840253 | 100000 | 430597.5282 | 330597.5282 | 12.4684741 | 4306 |
| 02-Feb-15 | | 359.808 | 0 | 1234.371779 | 100000 | 444136.841 | 344136.841 | 12.34269388 | 4441 |
| 02-Mar-15 | | 361.473 | 0 | 1222.029085 | 100000 | 441730.5194 | 341730.5194 | 12.21944654 | 4417 |
| 01-Apr-15 | | 346.246 | 0 | 1209.809638 | 100000 | 418891.7481 | 318891.7481 | 12.09833471 | 4189 |
| 04-May-15 | | 340.055 | 0 | 1197.711304 | 100000 | 407287.7174 | 307287.7174 | 11.97747423 | 4073 |
| 01-Jun-15 | | 342.512 | 0 | 1185.73383 | 100000 | 406128.0654 | 306128.0654 | 11.8565189 | 4061 |
| 01-Jul-15 | | 341.717 | 0 | 1173.877311 | 100000 | 401133.8329 | 301133.8329 | 11.73778302 | 4011 |
| 03-Aug-15 | | 352.187 | 0 | 1162.139528 | 100000 | 409290.4338 | 309290.4338 | 11.6216669 | 4093 |
| 01-Sep-15 | | 317.114 | 0 | 1150.517861 | 100000 | 364845.3209 | 264845.3209 | 11.50374944 | 3648 |
| 01-Oct-15 | | 322.533 | 0 | 1139.014111 | 100000 | 367369.6383 | 267369.6383 | 11.39108246 | 3674 |
| 02-Nov-15 | | 328.504 | 0 | 1127.623029 | 100000 | 370428.6754 | 270428.6754 | 11.27535738 | 3704 |
| 01-Dec-15 | | 330.806 | 0 | 1116.347671 | 100000 | 369294.5078 | 269294.5078 | 11.16364274 | 3693 |
| 01-Jan-16 | | 326.019 | 0 | 1105.184029 | 100000 | 360310.9918 | 260310.9918 | 11.05150313 | 3603 |
| 01-Feb-16 | | 296.937 | 0 | 1094.132526 | 100000 | 324888.4297 | 224888.4297 | 10.94171491 | 3249 |
| 01-Mar-16 | | 279.887 | 0 | 1083.190811 | 100000 | 303171.0264 | 203171.0264 | 10.83294329 | 3032 |
| **toatal** | **100000** | | | | | | | | **542931** |

# 5

# 24% Yearly Return from Share Genius SIP in Nifty

In this chapter, I'd like to share a research I had undertaken, in which you can earn up to 50% more returns by undertaking a Share Genius SIP rather than an ordinary SIP. However, in the practical example I've given, you will see returns of more than 24% per annum. But since returns are never guaranteed in the stock market, I cannot assure you that you will get returns of more than 24% per annum. But I have definitely proven from my research that this method is 50% more productive than the simple SIP.

Let's put it this way – when in a year you would have received only 14% returns from an ordinary SIP, by undertaking an SIP with this method, you would have received 50% more ie, about 21% returns.

Readers who are already following me on YouTube may have already seen a video of this method on my channel. Still, I advise you that even if you have already watched the YouTube video, do read this chapter carefully till the end, as a few readers expressed their doubts which I have answered. An advanced form of this method is being presented in this chapter, will only enlighten the readers further.

For this, you need to select Nifty 50 or Bank Nifty based good ETFs (Exchange Traded Fund) with sufficient value. Currently, the 5 ETFs with the highest volume based on Nifty 50 in the Indian stock markets are:

1. NIFTYBEES
2. SETNIF50
3. ICICINIFTY
4. KOTAKNIFTY
5. HDFCNIFETF

And the 5 ETFs based on Bank Nifty with the highest volume are:

1. BANKBEES
2. KOTAKBKETF
3. SETNIFBK
4. ABSLBANETF
5. ICICIBANKN

You can select any of the above ETFs for a monthly SIP.

I prefer investing in ETFs based on Nifty 50 vis-a-vis Bank Nifty because Nifty 50 has more shares (ie, it is more diversified) than Bank Nifty. Nifty 50 is based on different sectors, whereas Bank Nifty is based only on the banking sector and most of the shares of Bank Nifty are also included in Nifty 50.

The rest is your choice. You can also use this method for SIP in mutual funds other than ATF.

In this method, you can start an SIP on any date of any month. You will decide for yourself when to start the first installment and how much will be the amount of the first installment. After that, in the next month when you will buy the units according to the next instalment of SIP, then you have to first check what the profit or loss situation on the units that you bought last month was.

After this you have to adjust your next month's SIP amount according to the following three steps:

1. Calculate the profit and loss on the trailing holding as a percentage.
2. Multiply this percentage profit and loss by 4.
3. The figure that comes after multiplying by 4, reduce that percentage amount if your holding is in profit and increase if you are in loss.

If you have not understood anything after reading the above three points, you do not need to panic. I will explain everything through practical examples.

In the appendices given in this book, see Appendix-E. I have used KOTAKNIFTY statistics to explain that to you.

We will use the data in Appendix-E to understand what would have happened if we had invested in Share Genius SIP in KOTAKNIFTY ETF for 1 year from 1st September, 2019 to 30th August, 2020? What would have happened if we had made a lump sum investment or a simple SIP instead of a Share Genius SIP?

The calculation sheet in Appendix-F is given at the end of the book.

Now from the first instalment on 1st and 2nd September, 2019 from the close of the market, you bought the shares of KOTAKNIFTY on 3rd September, 2019. You had fixed 10,000 for the first installment. You decide the amount to be invested in SIP. But you have to decide only the amount for the first installment. After that my system will decide how much you will invest in the following months. Don't panic. Your average investment amount for 12 months will come to around ₹ 10,000 per month. The only difference is that with this system, when the market is bullish, your SIP amount will automatically reduce. When the market is in a downturn, your SIP amount will automatically increase.

So as per Appendix-F on 3rd September, 2019, you bought 89 shares of KOTAKNIFTY at the average price of 112.54 shares on that day and invested ₹ 10,016.06 as the 1st installment. (I have not included brokerage and taxes here to keep the calculation simple).

Now you have to decide the amount you want to invest on 1st October, 2019. For this, calculate the value of your investment at the closing price on September 30, 2019. Its closing price on that day was 119.46. Accordingly, the value of 89 shares held by you becomes 10,631.94, which is ₹ 615.88 more than your original investment of 10,016.06. That is, you are getting profit of ₹ 615.88 on your holding. When you convert this profit percentage in term, you are getting profit of ₹ 615.88 on ₹ 10,016.06 ie, approximately 6.15%.

Now, multiplying this 6.15% by 4 gives 24.60%. That is, we have to reduce the amount of new SIP by 24.60% from the previous amount. You can reduce it to an integer by 25%. So, on 1st October, you have to invest 25% less than 10,000, ie, you have to invets only ₹ 7500.

You will see in Appendix-F that as on 31st October, the total return on investment was 6.42%. Its 4 times is 25.70%. So, by reducing the whole number by 26%, the SIP of this month is obtained which is only ₹ 7,400. Similarly, on 31st January, 2020, due to a slight fall in the market, only 3.06%

profit was being made on the total investment. So, we reduced it to 4 times, that is, about 12% of the whole. So, instead of 10,000, we invested 12% less which was ₹ 8,800 only.

Now on 28th February, 2020, there was a loss of 3.50% on the total investment. So, we will increase the SIP amount by 4 times the percentage loss.

So, on 2nd March, 2020, we invested 11,400 by increasing the amount 4 times, the 14% of 3.50.

The worst situation we have faced was the time of lockdown of 31st March, 2020. During that time, you can see (in Appendix-E) that we were incurring a loss of 26.44%. So, we had to multiply the SIP amount by 4 times of 26.44 ie, 105.76%, rounding it of as 106%. That is, on 1st April, 2020, instead of 10,000, we invested 106% more ie, 20,600.

Similarly, on 30th April, 2020, when the loss was 7.54%, we increased its SIP by 4 times 30.19% (30% in integer) to 13,000.

Thus you can see that by this Share Genius SIP method we invested 1,24,229.78 in 12 months, and received a total profit of ₹ 15,616.81 which is 12.57% profit of the total invested amount 1,24,229.78.

But actually if we count the CAGR (Compound Annual Growth Rate) or in simple words the real interest, then this profit was more than 24% per annum not 12.57% because we had invested around ₹ 10,000 per month by not investing 1.24 lakh together. You will see in the table (Sheet 3 of E) how if you had invested 10,000 per month and earned 2% interest on it, then in a year you would have earned 15,600 with 24% compound interest.

The calculation of the compound interest rate is given in Appendix-H.

So even in this SIP, the actual CAGR is around 24% per annum.

Now let's talk about how much return would we get if we had invested simply ₹ 10,000 per month without worrying so much? As you can see in Appendix-G, you would have earned a profit of 10,059.63 instead of 15,616.18, which is a simple return of 8.39% or a compound return of 16%.

So, Share Genius SIP is 1.50 times more effective than a simple SIP.

Now let's talk about how much returns we would have received had we made a lump sum investment of 1.20 lakhs (12 months amounting to 10,000 per month) directly without an SIP?

If we had invested 1,20,000 in KOTAKNIFTY ETF on 3rd September, 2019 at a price of 112.54, then after 1 year on 28th August, 2020, it was trading at 120.83 per share. That is, if you would have got a profit of about 7.36% in 1 year, then according to the Compound Annual Growth Rate (CAGR), then in 1 year the CAGR would have been as follows:

1. 7.36% on lump sum investment
2. 16% on Simple Monthly SIP
3. 24% on Share Genius Monthly SIP

I hope you have got an idea of the power of Share Genius SIP. Now let us consider some common doubts. I'll discuss the solutions to the questions and doubts expressed by people on my channel.

Frequently asked questions about Share Genius SIP and their answers:

1. Mahesh sir, your method is absolutely illogical. If we invest in a long term SIP of 10-15 years, then there will come a time when the profit will be more than 25%. Then 4 times of 25 ie, more than 100% SIP amount will have to be reduced. So, in such a situation, the monthly installment will have to be stopped and if the profit is more than 30%, then the amount will have to be reduced by more than 100% (30 times 4 times 120). How is this possible?

**Answer:** This method is to be used for a maximum period of 12 months or whenever the total profit exceeds 25%. Whichever of the above events happens first, after that a new SIP has to be done by booking profit. That is, by this method, if you get more than 25% profit on the total investment in 8 months, then you can close it and book profit by selling the previous holding. You can keep starting a new SIP from the next month onward. Even if it has been 12 months and the total profit is only 12.47%, then you have to book a new SIP after every 12 months.

2. Sir, in this way I will be deprived of the benefits of a long-term SIP. I have heard that in a long term SIP, crores of rupees are made due to the power of compound interest. But you are booking profit in only 12 months. Then how will my fund of crores of rupees be made?

**Answer**: If you really want to do Share Genius SIP in the long term, then there is a method for that too. After 12 months, in the example given in Appendix-E, you recover a total amount of 1,39,725.72 in your SIP including profit of ₹ 15,495.94, then you invest this amount in a corporate bond fund.

Corporate Bond Fund is a type of debt fund on which one can easily get higher returns than bank FDs.

Now you have to withdraw 1/12 of this amount every month from the Corporate Bond Fund and invest it again with a new SIP.

Like in the example of Appendix-F, you get ₹ 1,39,725, you have to divide that amount into 12 parts and invest it again in the next 12 months with a new SIP.

The 12th of 1,39,725 is 11,643.75. On rounding it (rounded off to the nearest 100 rupees), it comes to ₹ 11,400. So, from next year onwards we will do Share Genius SIP of 21,600 per month instead of SIP of 10,000 by adding 11,600 per month to 10,000, which will also invest the previous profit booked in 12 months again.

The same process has to be repeated again by booking profits every year.

You will get double benefit from this. One, you will be able to take advantage of Genius SIP, which is 50% more powerful than an ordinary SIP. Second, the lump sum amount that you received by booking profit, you have to invest it in an open ended corporate bond fund and sell the amount by selling as many units as you need for Share Genius SIP for around ₹ 11,600 per month. The rest of the amount will continue to earn around 6 to 9% in your corporate bond fund. Corporate bond funds will be discussed in subsequent chapters.

3. Can I use this method with mutual funds instead of ETFs?

**Answer**: Yes, using this method you can invest in mutual funds instead of ETFs. There are also types of mutual funds which trade like shares on the stock exchange.

4. Can Share Genius SIP be used in Shares too?

**Answer:** Yes. ETFs are also a type of mutual fund that trade like shares on a stock exchange.Therefore, for wealth creation in the long term, instead of investing more money in a particular stock, you should invest more money in ETFs or mutual funds.

If you still want to invest a large amount of money in a stock through the SIP method, then you are advised to read my book *How Chandu earned and Chinki lost in the Stock Market*, where the method of making regular investments and withdrawal of 200 DMA in a particular share on the basis of SIP method has been explained.

5. Suppose after the completion of 1 year the market is quite down and we are incurring 5-10% loss instead of profit, should we book a loss after 1 year and get a new SIP even then?

**Answer**: No, we do not invest in a SIP to book the loss. After 1 year if your total profit is less than 12% (overall 12% profit on SIP in 1 year then CAGR is around 24%) then you can continue SIP of Share Genius method even after 1 year till at least 12% profit is being made on the amount invested in the SIP.

6. Whatever be the profit or loss, you ask us to increase or decrease in the next installment of the SIP, an amount equal to the percentage obtained by multiplying it by 4. But why should we multiply by 4? Can't we multiply by 2,3,5 or 6 instead of 4?

**Answer**: It is said that the knowledge that a guru acquires by hard work of 12 years, can be given to the disciple in 5 minutes. Actually, I am working on this method for many years. I have tried multiplying by different multipliers like 1, 1.5, 2, 2.5, 3, 3.5, 4, 4.5, 5. I have found that multiplying by a coefficient of 4 gives the best results. So, my advice is to multiply by 4.

7. Kaushik sir, this method of yours is absolutely rubbish. I back-tested the scores on the historical data of the Gold Seed ETF from April 2020 to April 2021. There was loss instead of a 24% return.

**Answer**: I am not saying that an SIP of this method will give you guaranteed 25% return. You know that investing in the stock market is always subject to market risk. If the market or ETF prices fall, this SIP will not give you magical returns. Gold Seed ETF is an ETF based on gold. In the last 1 year, its return has been zero to minus. That is, its NAV in April 2020 was around 41, which is also around 41 in April 2021. In between, on 6$^{th}$ August, 2020, its NAV also went up to 48. That is, it would have been a loss even in a normal SIP. Share Genius SIP can reduce the loss by up to 50% as compared to the normal SIP. But it cannot magically turn into profit.

Anyway, you should invest in Sovereign Gold Bonds instead of Gold ETFs. In this, the SIP has a different method, which will be explained to you in the next chapter.

## Summary

1. When the market is bullish, instead of an ordinary SIP, investment can be reduced comparatively with Share Genius SIP. When the market is down, the investment can be increased comparatively.
2. In Share Genius SIP, whenever 1 year is completed or 25% profit is being received, by investing the amount obtained by booking profit in a Corporate Bond Fund and increasing the amount of new SIP by as much as 1/12 of the amount received, you create such a balanced system of equity and debt funds which is safer and gives higher returns than ordinary SIPs.

# APPENDIX-E

| Symbol | Series | Date | Prev Close | Open Price | High Price | Low Price | Last Price | Close Price | Average Price | Investment | share buy at average price | total investment | Total Share | Value at Close |
|---|---|---|---|---|---|---|---|---|---|---|---|---|---|---|
| KOTAKNIFTY | EQ | 30-Aug-19 | 113.98 | 113.95 | 114.4 | 112.75 | 113.71 | 113.58 | 113.28 | | | | | |
| KOTAKNIFTY | EQ | 03-Sep-19 | 113.58 | 111.3 | 113.42 | 111 | 111.89 | 111.82 | 112.54 | 10016.06 | 89 | 10016.06 | 89 | 9951.98 |
| KOTAKNIFTY | EQ | 04-Sep-19 | 111.82 | 112 | 112.81 | 111.68 | 112.6 | 112.5 | 112.14 | | | | | |
| KOTAKNIFTY | EQ | 05-Sep-19 | 112.5 | 112.81 | 113.3 | 111.98 | 112.25 | 112.41 | 112.69 | | | | | |
| KOTAKNIFTY | EQ | 06-Sep-19 | 112.41 | 112.5 | 113.35 | 112.1 | 112.9 | 112.9 | 112.89 | | | | | |
| KOTAKNIFTY | EQ | 09-Sep-19 | 112.9 | 113 | 114.19 | 112.4 | 113.3 | 113.52 | 113.59 | | | | | |
| KOTAKNIFTY | EQ | 11-Sep-19 | 113.52 | 114.05 | 114.45 | 113.5 | 114.24 | 114.22 | 114.02 | | | | | |
| KOTAKNIFTY | EQ | 12-Sep-19 | 114.22 | 114 | 114.9 | 113.7 | 113.7 | 113.72 | 114.51 | | | | | |
| KOTAKNIFTY | EQ | 13-Sep-19 | 113.72 | 113.72 | 114.5 | 113.05 | 114.35 | 114.33 | 113.63 | | | | | |
| KOTAKNIFTY | EQ | 16-Sep-19 | 114.33 | 114.27 | 114.49 | 113.46 | 113.75 | 113.95 | 113.99 | | | | | |
| KOTAKNIFTY | EQ | 17-Sep-19 | 113.95 | 113.5 | 113.86 | 111.85 | 111.9 | 112.15 | 112.77 | | | | | |
| KOTAKNIFTY | EQ | 18-Sep-19 | 112.15 | 112.7 | 112.85 | 111.9 | 112.67 | 112.26 | 112.34 | | | | | |
| KOTAKNIFTY | EQ | 19-Sep-19 | 112.26 | 112.35 | 112.4 | 110.94 | 111.1 | 111.07 | 111.2 | | | | | |
| KOTAKNIFTY | EQ | 20-Sep-19 | 111.07 | 113 | 117.4 | 110.8 | 116.5 | 116.37 | 115.08 | | | | | |
| KOTAKNIFTY | EQ | 23-Sep-19 | 116.37 | 120 | 125 | 118 | 121.5 | 120.59 | 121.62 | 30 Sep value at close | | 10631.94 | | |
| KOTAKNIFTY | EQ | 24-Sep-19 | 120.59 | 120.59 | 123 | 119.31 | 119.8 | 119.93 | 121.28 | Basic Value | | 10016.06 | | |
| KOTAKNIFTY | EQ | 25-Sep-19 | 119.93 | 118.55 | 119.95 | 118.55 | 118.8 | 118.88 | 119 | Profit / Loss | | 615.88 | | |
| KOTAKNIFTY | EQ | 26-Sep-19 | 118.88 | 119.2 | 120.25 | 119.2 | 119.6 | 119.62 | 119.51 | Profit in percentage | | 6.148924827 | | |
| KOTAKNIFTY | EQ | 27-Sep-19 | 119.62 | 120 | 120.15 | 119.3 | 119.3 | 119.52 | 119.8 | Four Time Adjustment % | | -24.59569931 | | |
| KOTAKNIFTY | EQ | 30-Sep-19 | 119.52 | 119.56 | 119.7 | 118.23 | 119.65 | 119.46 | 119.29 | Next SIP Amount | | 7500 | | |
| KOTAKNIFTY | EQ | 01-Oct-19 | 119.46 | 119.51 | 120 | 117 | 117.6 | 117.49 | 118.77 | 7482.51 | 63 | 17498.57 | 152 | 17858.48 |
| KOTAKNIFTY | EQ | 03-Oct-19 | 117.49 | 117.01 | 117.79 | 116.5 | 117.2 | 117.08 | 117.13 | | | | | |
| KOTAKNIFTY | EQ | 04-Oct-19 | 117.08 | 117.4 | 117.9 | 115.95 | 116.04 | 116.03 | 116.96 | | | | | |
| KOTAKNIFTY | EQ | 07-Oct-19 | 116.03 | 116.15 | 116.7 | 115.36 | 115.65 | 115.82 | 116.33 | | | | | |
| KOTAKNIFTY | EQ | 09-Oct-19 | 115.82 | 118.1 | 128.6 | 115.25 | 117.39 | 116.97 | 115.91 | | | | | |
| KOTAKNIFTY | EQ | 10-Oct-19 | 116.97 | 116.82 | 117.08 | 116.06 | 116.51 | 116.45 | 116.43 | | | | | |
| KOTAKNIFTY | EQ | 11-Oct-19 | 116.45 | 116.69 | 117.47 | 115.81 | 116.98 | 116.7 | 116.64 | | | | | |
| KOTAKNIFTY | EQ | 14-Oct-19 | 116.7 | 117 | 117.9 | 116.8 | 117.6 | 117.31 | 117.31 | | | | | |
| KOTAKNIFTY | EQ | 15-Oct-19 | 117.31 | 117.6 | 118.4 | 117.3 | 117.91 | 118 | 117.61 | | | | | |
| KOTAKNIFTY | EQ | 16-Oct-19 | 118 | 115.6 | 118.7 | 105 | 118.5 | 118.18 | 118.31 | | | | | |
| KOTAKNIFTY | EQ | 17-Oct-19 | 118.18 | 118.02 | 119.64 | 118.02 | 119.64 | 119.49 | 118.88 | | | | | |
| KOTAKNIFTY | EQ | 18-Oct-19 | 119.49 | 118.95 | 121 | 118.95 | 120.55 | 120.36 | 120.36 | | | | | |

| | | | | | | | | | |
|---|---|---|---|---|---|---|---|---|---|
| KOTAKNIFTY | EQ | 22-Oct-19 | 120.36 | 120.61 | 121 | 119.75 | 120.25 | 119.98 | 120.36 |
| KOTAKNIFTY | EQ | 23-Oct-19 | 119.98 | 120 | 120.5 | 119.5 | 119.51 | 119.6 | 119.86 |
| KOTAKNIFTY | EQ | 24-Oct-19 | 119.6 | 120.06 | 120.78 | 119.5 | 120 | 119.91 | 120.23 |
| KOTAKNIFTY | EQ | 25-Oct-19 | 119.91 | 119.99 | 120.6 | 119.5 | 120.5 | 120.34 | 119.7 |
| KOTAKNIFTY | EQ | 27-Oct-19 | 120.34 | 121.11 | 121.11 | 119.91 | 120.6 | 120.29 | 120.25 |
| KOTAKNIFTY | EQ | 29-Oct-19 | 120.29 | 120.16 | 122 | 120.12 | 121.54 | 121.74 | 121.55 |
| KOTAKNIFTY | EQ | 30-Oct-19 | 121.74 | 121.7 | 122.68 | 121.7 | 122 | 122.12 | 122.15 |
| KOTAKNIFTY | EQ | 31-Oct-19 | 122.12 | 122.39 | 123.2 | 122.2 | 122.33 | 122.52 | 122.7 |
| KOTAKNIFTY | EQ | 01-Nov-19 | 122.52 | 122.5 | 123.68 | 122.26 | 122.8 | 122.84 | 122.82 |
| KOTAKNIFTY | EQ | 04-Nov-19 | 122.84 | 123.17 | 123.89 | 122.49 | 123.45 | 123.28 | 123.27 |
| KOTAKNIFTY | EQ | 05-Nov-19 | 123.28 | 123.1 | 123.55 | 122.6 | 123.25 | 123.22 | 123.23 |
| KOTAKNIFTY | EQ | 06-Nov-19 | 123.22 | 123 | 124 | 122.56 | 123.46 | 123.59 | 123.54 |
| KOTAKNIFTY | EQ | 07-Nov-19 | 123.59 | 123.6 | 124.3 | 123.5 | 124.11 | 124 | 123.88 |
| KOTAKNIFTY | EQ | 08-Nov-19 | 124 | 123.8 | 124.65 | 123 | 123.2 | 123.27 | 123.69 |
| KOTAKNIFTY | EQ | 11-Nov-19 | 123.27 | 123.11 | 123.72 | 122.47 | 123.09 | 123.19 | 123.08 |
| KOTAKNIFTY | EQ | 13-Nov-19 | 123.19 | 123.39 | 123.55 | 122.17 | 122.68 | 122.34 | 122.94 |
| KOTAKNIFTY | EQ | 14-Nov-19 | 122.34 | 122.68 | 123 | 121.9 | 122.5 | 122.48 | 122.49 |
| KOTAKNIFTY | EQ | 15-Nov-19 | 122.48 | 124.9 | 125 | 122.52 | 123.07 | 123.09 | 123.01 |
| KOTAKNIFTY | EQ | 18-Nov-19 | 123.09 | 123.31 | 123.32 | 122.74 | 122.9 | 122.77 | 122.95 |
| KOTAKNIFTY | EQ | 19-Nov-19 | 122.77 | 123.3 | 123.5 | 122.55 | 123.5 | 123.36 | 123.17 |
| KOTAKNIFTY | EQ | 20-Nov-19 | 123.36 | 120.9 | 125.8 | 109.8 | 123.6 | 123.78 | 123.91 |
| KOTAKNIFTY | EQ | 21-Nov-19 | 123.78 | 124 | 124.4 | 122.15 | 124.01 | 123.9 | 123.82 |
| KOTAKNIFTY | EQ | 22-Nov-19 | 123.9 | 123.9 | 123.9 | 122.9 | 123.43 | 122.99 | 123.44 |
| KOTAKNIFTY | EQ | 25-Nov-19 | 122.99 | 123.23 | 124.62 | 122.92 | 124.56 | 124.57 | 124.34 |
| KOTAKNIFTY | EQ | 26-Nov-19 | 124.57 | 124.65 | 124.95 | 124.04 | 124.59 | 124.74 | 124.78 |
| KOTAKNIFTY | EQ | 27-Nov-19 | 124.74 | 124.62 | 124.97 | 124.6 | 124.75 | 124.86 | 124.82 |
| KOTAKNIFTY | EQ | 28-Nov-19 | 124.86 | 124.74 | 126.45 | 124.74 | 126.32 | 126.3 | 125.88 |
| KOTAKNIFTY | EQ | 29-Nov-19 | 126.3 | 126.22 | 126.22 | 124.8 | 125.45 | 125.34 | 125.29 |
| KOTAKNIFTY | EQ | 02-Dec-19 | 125.34 | 124.81 | 125.56 | 123.75 | 125.08 | 125.01 | 125.02 |
| KOTAKNIFTY | EQ | 03-Dec-19 | 125.01 | 125.05 | 125.05 | 123.67 | 124.25 | 124.19 | 124.26 |
| KOTAKNIFTY | EQ | 04-Dec-19 | 124.19 | 126.7 | 129.2 | 123.7 | 125.03 | 124.75 | 124.31 |
| KOTAKNIFTY | EQ | 05-Dec-19 | 124.75 | 125.99 | 125.99 | 124.02 | 124.18 | 124.28 | 124.59 |
| KOTAKNIFTY | EQ | 06-Dec-19 | 124.28 | 124.77 | 124.8 | 123.65 | 123.95 | 124.25 | 124.24 |
| KOTAKNIFTY | EQ | 09-Dec-19 | 124.25 | 126.7 | 129.2 | 123.5 | 123.95 | 123.94 | 123.92 |

| | | | | |
|---|---|---|---|---|
| 31 Oct value at close | | 18623.04 | | |
| Basic Value | | 17498.57 | | |
| Profit / Loss | | 1124.47 | | |
| Profit in percentage | | 6.426067959 | | |
| Four Time Adjustment % | | -25.70427183 | | |
| Next SIP Amount | | 7400 | | |
| 7369.2 | 60 | 24867.77 | 212 | 26042.08 |

| | | | | |
|---|---|---|---|---|
| 29 Nov value at close | | 26572.08 | | |
| Basic Value | | 24867.77 | | |
| Profit / Loss | | 1704.31 | | |
| Profit in percentage | | 6.853489477 | | |
| Four Time Adjustment % | | -27.41395791 | | |
| Next SIP Amount | | 7300 | | |
| 7251.16 | 58 | 32118.93 | 269 | 33627.69 |

| | | | | | | | | | | | | | | |
|---|---|---|---|---|---|---|---|---|---|---|---|---|---|---|
| KOTAKNIFTY | EQ | 10-Dec-19 | 123.94 | 125.9 | 125.9 | 122.58 | 123.46 | 123.21 | 123.19 | | | | | |
| KOTAKNIFTY | EQ | 11-Dec-19 | 123.21 | 124 | 124 | 122.8 | 123.2 | 123.11 | 123.2 | | | | | |
| KOTAKNIFTY | EQ | 12-Dec-19 | 123.11 | 123.11 | 124.57 | 123.11 | 123.94 | 123.95 | 123.96 | | | | | |
| KOTAKNIFTY | EQ | 13-Dec-19 | 123.95 | 124.24 | 125.45 | 124.21 | 125.4 | 125.12 | 124.78 | | | | | |
| KOTAKNIFTY | EQ | 16-Dec-19 | 125.12 | 125 | 125.48 | 124.6 | 124.75 | 124.77 | 125.01 | | | | | |
| KOTAKNIFTY | EQ | 17-Dec-19 | 124.77 | 124.8 | 125.86 | 124.8 | 125.83 | 125.73 | 125.44 | | | | | |
| KOTAKNIFTY | EQ | 18-Dec-19 | 125.73 | 125.95 | 126.3 | 125.56 | 126.3 | 126.15 | 125.93 | | | | | |
| KOTAKNIFTY | EQ | 19-Dec-19 | 126.15 | 126.35 | 126.5 | 125.72 | 126.5 | 126.39 | 126.18 | | | | | |
| KOTAKNIFTY | EQ | 20-Dec-19 | 126.39 | 126.39 | 126.78 | 126.39 | 126.4 | 126.49 | 126.51 | | | | | |
| KOTAKNIFTY | EQ | 23-Dec-19 | 126.49 | 140.4 | 149.3 | 126.1 | 126.6 | 126.44 | 126.47 | 31 Dec value at close | | 34114.58 | | |
| KOTAKNIFTY | EQ | 24-Dec-19 | 126.44 | 126.4 | 126.97 | 126.1 | 126.45 | 126.37 | 126.6 | Basic Value | | 32118.93 | | |
| KOTAKNIFTY | EQ | 26-Dec-19 | 126.37 | 127.39 | 127.39 | 125.05 | 125.52 | 125.4 | 125.71 | Profit / Loss | | 1995.65 | | |
| KOTAKNIFTY | EQ | 27-Dec-19 | 125.4 | 125.5 | 127 | 125.2 | 126.54 | 126.56 | 126.01 | Profit in percentage | | 6.21331408 | | |
| KOTAKNIFTY | EQ | 30-Dec-19 | 126.56 | 129.1 | 130 | 126.49 | 127.25 | 127.46 | 127.33 | 4x Adjustment % | | -24.85325632 | | |
| KOTAKNIFTY | EQ | 31-Dec-19 | 127.46 | 126.6 | 127.46 | 126.25 | 126.95 | 126.82 | 126.74 | Next SIP Amount | | 7400 | | |
| KOTAKNIFTY | EQ | 01-Jan-20 | 126.82 | 127.79 | 130 | 125.89 | 126.35 | 126.47 | 126.49 | 7462.91 | 59 | 39581.84 | 328 | 41488.72 |
| KOTAKNIFTY | EQ | 02-Jan-20 | 126.47 | 135.3 | 135.3 | 126.41 | 127.2 | 127.01 | 126.91 | | | | | |
| KOTAKNIFTY | EQ | 03-Jan-20 | 127.01 | 127.01 | 132.46 | 126.14 | 126.44 | 126.33 | 128.39 | | | | | |
| KOTAKNIFTY | EQ | 06-Jan-20 | 126.33 | 126 | 126.38 | 124.45 | 124.7 | 124.65 | 125.28 | | | | | |
| KOTAKNIFTY | EQ | 07-Jan-20 | 124.65 | 124.71 | 126.3 | 124.71 | 125.2 | 125.24 | 125.48 | | | | | |
| KOTAKNIFTY | EQ | 08-Jan-20 | 125.24 | 125.24 | 125.24 | 123.91 | 124.65 | 124.82 | 124.38 | | | | | |
| KOTAKNIFTY | EQ | 09-Jan-20 | 124.82 | 125.59 | 126.74 | 125.55 | 126.45 | 126.47 | 126.42 | | | | | |
| KOTAKNIFTY | EQ | 10-Jan-20 | 126.47 | 127.05 | 127.5 | 126.45 | 126.7 | 126.72 | 127.21 | | | | | |
| KOTAKNIFTY | EQ | 13-Jan-20 | 126.72 | 127.14 | 127.69 | 127.14 | 127.64 | 127.5 | 127.45 | | | | | |
| KOTAKNIFTY | EQ | 14-Jan-20 | 127.5 | 128.5 | 128.5 | 127.28 | 127.87 | 127.87 | 127.63 | | | | | |
| KOTAKNIFTY | EQ | 15-Jan-20 | 127.87 | 127.7 | 128 | 127.2 | 128 | 127.98 | 127.63 | | | | | |
| KOTAKNIFTY | EQ | 16-Jan-20 | 127.98 | 136.9 | 139.5 | 116.5 | 127.8 | 127.84 | 128.11 | | | | | |
| KOTAKNIFTY | EQ | 17-Jan-20 | 127.84 | 127.84 | 128.34 | 127.48 | 127.81 | 128.09 | 128.04 | | | | | |
| KOTAKNIFTY | EQ | 20-Jan-20 | 128.09 | 128.09 | 128.09 | 126.91 | 127.24 | 127.02 | 127.44 | | | | | |
| KOTAKNIFTY | EQ | 21-Jan-20 | 127.02 | 127.02 | 127.07 | 126.05 | 126.2 | 126.25 | 126.61 | | | | | |
| KOTAKNIFTY | EQ | 22-Jan-20 | 126.25 | 126.95 | 126.95 | 125.5 | 125.86 | 125.74 | 126.07 | | | | | |
| KOTAKNIFTY | EQ | 23-Jan-20 | 125.74 | 125.95 | 126.61 | 125.4 | 126.5 | 126.35 | 126.26 | | | | | |
| KOTAKNIFTY | EQ | 24-Jan-20 | 126.35 | 126.07 | 127.4 | 125.79 | 127.4 | 127.33 | 127.18 | 31 Jan value at close | | 40672 | | |
| KOTAKNIFTY | EQ | 27-Jan-20 | 127.33 | 126.53 | 126.95 | 125.65 | 126.2 | 126.09 | 126.36 | Basic Value | | 39581.84 | | |

| | | | | | | | | | | | | | | |
|---|---|---|---|---|---|---|---|---|---|---|---|---|---|---|
| KOTAKNIFTY | EQ | 28-Jan-20 | 126.09 | 127.38 | 127.38 | 125 | 125.53 | 125.27 | 125.52 | Profit / Loss | | 1090.16 | | |
| KOTAKNIFTY | EQ | 29-Jan-20 | 125.27 | 125.9 | 126.29 | 125.02 | 125.89 | 125.68 | 125.7 | Profit in percentage | | 2.754192327 | | |
| KOTAKNIFTY | EQ | 30-Jan-20 | 125.68 | 125.4 | 125.65 | 124.6 | 125.25 | 125.36 | 125.22 | 4x Adjustment % | | -11.01676931 | | |
| KOTAKNIFTY | EQ | 31-Jan-20 | 125.36 | 125.5 | 125.54 | 123.99 | 124.21 | 124 | 124.5 | Next SIP Amount | | 8800 | | |
| KOTAKNIFTY | EQ | 01-Feb-20 | 124 | 123.81 | 125 | 122.31 | 122.6 | 122.77 | 124.32 | 8826.72 | 71 | 48408.56 | 399 | 48985.23 |
| KOTAKNIFTY | EQ | 03-Feb-20 | 122.77 | 121.64 | 122.18 | 121.1 | 121.7 | 121.33 | 121.7 | | | | | |
| KOTAKNIFTY | EQ | 04-Feb-20 | 121.33 | 123.48 | 124.5 | 122 | 124.4 | 124.38 | 124.03 | | | | | |
| KOTAKNIFTY | EQ | 05-Feb-20 | 124.38 | 124.4 | 125.5 | 124 | 125.5 | 125.25 | 124.82 | | | | | |
| KOTAKNIFTY | EQ | 06-Feb-20 | 125.25 | 125.31 | 125.95 | 125.14 | 125.5 | 125.6 | 125.51 | | | | | |
| KOTAKNIFTY | EQ | 07-Feb-20 | 125.6 | 125.12 | 125.95 | 125.01 | 125.45 | 125.44 | 125.43 | | | | | |
| KOTAKNIFTY | EQ | 10-Feb-20 | 125.44 | 125.44 | 125.44 | 124.16 | 124.95 | 124.69 | 124.72 | | | | | |
| KOTAKNIFTY | EQ | 11-Feb-20 | 124.69 | 124.89 | 126.15 | 124.89 | 125.45 | 125.48 | 125.55 | | | | | |
| KOTAKNIFTY | EQ | 12-Feb-20 | 125.48 | 126 | 128.7 | 125.9 | 126.55 | 126.6 | 127.77 | | | | | |
| KOTAKNIFTY | EQ | 13-Feb-20 | 126.6 | 126.55 | 126.55 | 125.72 | 126.25 | 126.01 | 125.91 | | | | | |
| KOTAKNIFTY | EQ | 14-Feb-20 | 126.01 | 126.9 | 126.9 | 125.1 | 125.49 | 125.29 | 126.09 | | | | | |
| KOTAKNIFTY | EQ | 17-Feb-20 | 125.29 | 131.8 | 131.8 | 124.73 | 125.28 | 125.2 | 125.24 | | | | | |
| KOTAKNIFTY | EQ | 18-Feb-20 | 125.2 | 124.7 | 124.79 | 123.77 | 124.63 | 124.41 | 124.24 | | | | | |
| KOTAKNIFTY | EQ | 19-Feb-20 | 124.41 | 125.35 | 125.74 | 124.76 | 125.72 | 125.69 | 125.07 | | | | | |
| KOTAKNIFTY | EQ | 20-Feb-20 | 125.69 | 125.69 | 125.75 | 125.04 | 125.5 | 125.44 | 125.62 | 28 Feb value at close | | 46595.22 | | |
| KOTAKNIFTY | EQ | 24-Feb-20 | 125.44 | 127.9 | 130.5 | 122.75 | 123.4 | 123.09 | 123.71 | Basic Value | | 48408.56 | | |
| KOTAKNIFTY | EQ | 25-Feb-20 | 123.09 | 123.1 | 123.5 | 122.48 | 122.75 | 122.56 | 123.04 | Profit / Loss | | -1813.34 | | |
| KOTAKNIFTY | EQ | 26-Feb-20 | 122.56 | 122 | 122.3 | 120.77 | 121.68 | 121.39 | 121.63 | Profit in percentage | | | -3.745907749 | |
| | | | | | | | | | | | | | | |
| KOTAKNIFTY | EQ | 27-Feb-20 | 121.39 | 121.2 | 121.2 | 120.15 | 120.74 | 120.55 | 120.51 | 4x Adjustment % | | 14.98363099 | | |
| KOTAKNIFTY | EQ | 28-Feb-20 | 120.55 | 119.5 | 119.5 | 116.15 | 118 | 116.78 | 117.53 | Next SIP Amount | | 11400 | | |
| KOTAKNIFTY | EQ | 02-Mar-20 | 116.78 | 118.28 | 118.59 | 116.23 | 116.72 | 116.79 | 117.6 | 11407.2 | 97 | 59815.76 | 496 | 57927.84 |
| KOTAKNIFTY | EQ | 03-Mar-20 | 116.79 | 119.1 | 121.5 | 116.15 | 117.45 | 117.43 | 116.95 | | | | | |
| KOTAKNIFTY | EQ | 04-Mar-20 | 117.43 | 117.34 | 117.78 | 115.5 | 117 | 116.87 | 116.56 | | | | | |
| KOTAKNIFTY | EQ | 05-Mar-20 | 116.87 | 119.2 | 119.2 | 116.93 | 117.02 | 117.13 | 117.37 | | | | | |
| KOTAKNIFTY | EQ | 06-Mar-20 | 117.13 | 119.5 | 121.8 | 112.6 | 114.2 | 114.83 | 114.47 | | | | | |
| KOTAKNIFTY | EQ | 09-Mar-20 | 114.83 | 117.1 | 119.4 | 108.1 | 109 | 109.95 | 110.04 | | | | | |
| KOTAKNIFTY | EQ | 11-Mar-20 | 109.95 | 109.95 | 109.95 | 107.96 | 109.11 | 109.16 | 108.89 | | | | | |
| KOTAKNIFTY | EQ | 12-Mar-20 | 109.16 | 109.16 | 109.16 | 100.2 | 102 | 101.83 | 103.38 | | | | | |
| KOTAKNIFTY | EQ | 13-Mar-20 | 101.83 | 110 | 110 | 93.1 | 105.1 | 104.73 | 100.07 | | | | | |

| KOTAKNIFTY | EQ | 16-Mar-20 | 104.73 | 104.73 | 104.73 | 95.9 | 96.35 | 96.58 | 98.6 | | | | | |
|---|---|---|---|---|---|---|---|---|---|---|---|---|---|---|
| KOTAKNIFTY | EQ | 17-Mar-20 | 96.58 | 123.96 | 123.96 | 94 | 96.8 | 95.29 | 96.63 | | | | | |
| KOTAKNIFTY | EQ | 18-Mar-20 | 95.29 | 97 | 97 | 89.95 | 90 | 90.45 | 91.85 | | | | | |
| KOTAKNIFTY | EQ | 19-Mar-20 | 90.45 | 90.45 | 91.97 | 85.15 | 86.5 | 86.26 | 87.19 | | | | | |
| KOTAKNIFTY | EQ | 20-Mar-20 | 86.26 | 88.49 | 91.41 | 85.25 | 90 | 89.96 | 89.42 | | | | | |
| KOTAKNIFTY | EQ | 23-Mar-20 | 89.96 | 85 | 87 | 81.01 | 83 | 82.09 | 82.71 | | | | | |
| KOTAKNIFTY | EQ | 24-Mar-20 | 82.09 | 88 | 101 | 81.95 | 84.4 | 84.04 | 84.42 | 31 Mar value at close | | 43910.88 | | |
| KOTAKNIFTY | EQ | 25-Mar-20 | 84.04 | 84.1 | 87 | 82.2 | 85.8 | 86.22 | 84.7 | Basic Value | | 59815.76 | | |
| KOTAKNIFTY | EQ | 26-Mar-20 | 86.22 | 86.22 | 90.9 | 85.5 | 88.99 | 89.39 | 89.19 | Profit / Loss | | -15904.88 | | |
| KOTAKNIFTY | EQ | 27-Mar-20 | 89.39 | 89.4 | 94.5 | 88.5 | 89.6 | 90.01 | 91.25 | Profit in percentage | | -26.58978169 | | |
| KOTAKNIFTY | EQ | 30-Mar-20 | 90.01 | 88.2 | 89 | 86.15 | 86.5 | 86.62 | 87.52 | 4x Adjustment % | | 106.3591268 | | |
| KOTAKNIFTY | EQ | 31-Mar-20 | 86.62 | 87.99 | 89.75 | 87 | 88.4 | 88.53 | 88.5 | Next SIP Amount | | 20600 | | |
| KOTAKNIFTY | EQ | 01-Apr-20 | 88.53 | 88.5 | 90 | 86.2 | 86.7 | 86.72 | 87.13 | 20562.68 | 236 | 80378.44 | 732 | 63479.04 |
| KOTAKNIFTY | EQ | 03-Apr-20 | 86.72 | 86.72 | 87.44 | 84 | 84.71 | 84.58 | 84.77 | | | | | |
| KOTAKNIFTY | EQ | 07-Apr-20 | 84.58 | 87.99 | 90.95 | 86 | 90.8 | 90.66 | 88.58 | | | | | |
| KOTAKNIFTY | EQ | 08-Apr-20 | 90.66 | 90.5 | 94.38 | 88.81 | 91.18 | 91.02 | 91.84 | | | | | |
| KOTAKNIFTY | EQ | 09-Apr-20 | 91.02 | 93.8 | 94.2 | 91.5 | 93.99 | 93.58 | 93.27 | | | | | |
| KOTAKNIFTY | EQ | 13-Apr-20 | 93.58 | 93.99 | 94.25 | 92.13 | 93.65 | 93.67 | 93.41 | | | | | |
| KOTAKNIFTY | EQ | 15-Apr-20 | 93.67 | 95.49 | 96 | 92.5 | 93.2 | 93.23 | 94.99 | | | | | |
| KOTAKNIFTY | EQ | 16-Apr-20 | 93.23 | 92.94 | 94.24 | 91.71 | 93.85 | 93.85 | 93.61 | | | | | |
| KOTAKNIFTY | EQ | 17-Apr-20 | 93.85 | 97.6 | 97.6 | 93.67 | 95.75 | 95.21 | 95.49 | | | | | |
| KOTAKNIFTY | EQ | 20-Apr-20 | 95.21 | 96.59 | 96.65 | 95.35 | 96.1 | 96.12 | 96.13 | | | | | |
| KOTAKNIFTY | EQ | 21-Apr-20 | 96.12 | 96 | 96 | 92.88 | 93.2 | 93.39 | 93.81 | | | | | |
| KOTAKNIFTY | EQ | 22-Apr-20 | 93.39 | 93.4 | 95.45 | 92.8 | 94.9 | 95.05 | 94.61 | | | | | |
| KOTAKNIFTY | EQ | 23-Apr-20 | 95.05 | 95.45 | 96.95 | 94.8 | 96.07 | 96.31 | 96.19 | 30 Apr value at close | | 74210.16 | | |
| KOTAKNIFTY | EQ | 24-Apr-20 | 96.31 | 96.5 | 96.5 | 94.72 | 95.24 | 94.98 | 95.23 | Basic Value | | 80378.44 | | |
| KOTAKNIFTY | EQ | 27-Apr-20 | 94.98 | 96.1 | 96.98 | 95.86 | 96.5 | 96.42 | 96.58 | Profit / Loss | | -6168.28 | | |
| KOTAKNIFTY | EQ | 28-Apr-20 | 96.42 | 97 | 97.39 | 95.95 | 97.02 | 96.91 | 96.2 | Profit in percentage | | -7.674047916 | | |
| KOTAKNIFTY | EQ | 29-Apr-20 | 96.91 | 97.61 | 99.6 | 97.06 | 99.11 | 99.24 | 98.51 | 4x Adjustment % | | 30.69619167 | | |
| KOTAKNIFTY | EQ | 30-Apr-20 | 99.24 | 103.2 | 108.2 | 99.5 | 101.21 | 101.38 | 101.42 | Next SIP Amount | | 13000 | | |
| KOTAKNIFTY | EQ | 04-May-20 | 101.38 | 98.88 | 98.88 | 96 | 96.68 | 96.56 | 96.95 | 12991.3 | 134 | 93369.74 | 866 | 83620.96 |
| KOTAKNIFTY | EQ | 05-May-20 | 96.56 | 99.5 | 102.4 | 95.5 | 96 | 95.78 | 96.79 | | | | | |
| KOTAKNIFTY | EQ | 06-May-20 | 95.78 | 95.78 | 96.75 | 94.75 | 96.2 | 95.9 | 95.97 | | | | | |
| KOTAKNIFTY | EQ | 07-May-20 | 95.9 | 95.3 | 96 | 94.67 | 95.68 | 95.41 | 95.31 | | | | | |

| | | | | | | | | | | | | | |
|---|---|---|---|---|---|---|---|---|---|---|---|---|---|
| KOTAKNIFTY | EQ | 08-May-20 | 95.41 | 96.7 | 97.02 | 95.59 | 96.13 | 95.91 | 96.36 | | | | |
| KOTAKNIFTY | EQ | 11-May-20 | 95.91 | 95.91 | 97.75 | 95.5 | 95.88 | 95.77 | 96.89 | | | | |
| KOTAKNIFTY | EQ | 12-May-20 | 95.77 | 95.3 | 96.1 | 94 | 95.92 | 95.62 | 94.8 | | | | |
| KOTAKNIFTY | EQ | 13-May-20 | 95.62 | 99 | 99.41 | 97.21 | 97.25 | 97.5 | 97.91 | | | | |
| KOTAKNIFTY | EQ | 14-May-20 | 97.5 | 96.6 | 96.6 | 95.06 | 95.65 | 95.58 | 95.69 | | | | |
| KOTAKNIFTY | EQ | 15-May-20 | 95.58 | 96 | 96 | 94 | 94.93 | 94.96 | 94.49 | | | | |
| KOTAKNIFTY | EQ | 18-May-20 | 94.96 | 95 | 95 | 91.73 | 92.28 | 91.9 | 92.47 | | | | |
| KOTAKNIFTY | EQ | 19-May-20 | 91.9 | 93 | 93.96 | 92.2 | 92.51 | 92.58 | 92.92 | | | | |
| KOTAKNIFTY | EQ | 20-May-20 | 92.58 | 92.58 | 94.6 | 92.5 | 94.6 | 94.15 | 93.31 | | | | |
| KOTAKNIFTY | EQ | 21-May-20 | 94.15 | 94.45 | 95.15 | 94.05 | 94.57 | 94.56 | 94.6 | 29 May value at close | | 85846.58 | |
| KOTAKNIFTY | EQ | 22-May-20 | 94.56 | 94.01 | 95 | 93.5 | 94.09 | 93.86 | 93.92 | Basic Value | | 93369.74 | |
| KOTAKNIFTY | EQ | 26-May-20 | 93.86 | 94.9 | 95.2 | 93.7 | 93.99 | 94.08 | 94.5 | Profit / Loss | | -7523.16 | |
| KOTAKNIFTY | EQ | 27-May-20 | 94.08 | 94.9 | 96.5 | 93.7 | 96.4 | 96.22 | 95.23 | Profit in percentage | | -8.057385616 | |
| KOTAKNIFTY | EQ | 28-May-20 | 96.22 | 96 | 98 | 96 | 97.8 | 97.85 | 97.45 | 4x Adjustment | | 32.22954246 | |
| KOTAKNIFTY | EQ | 29-May-20 | 97.85 | 97.5 | 99.5 | 97 | 99.24 | 99.13 | 98.01 | Next SIP Amount | | | 13200 |
| KOTAKNIFTY | EQ | 01-Jun-20 | 99.13 | 99.6 | 102.79 | 99.6 | 101.73 | 101.61 | 101.83 | 13237.9 | 130 | 106607.64 | 996 |
| 101422.68 | | | | | | | | | | | | | |
| KOTAKNIFTY | EQ | 02-Jun-20 | 101.61 | 102 | 103.4 | 101.52 | 103.28 | 103.18 | 102.63 | | | | |
| KOTAKNIFTY | EQ | 03-Jun-20 | 103.18 | 103.5 | 107 | 103.5 | 104.01 | 104.03 | 104.88 | | | | |
| KOTAKNIFTY | EQ | 04-Jun-20 | 104.03 | 104.35 | 105 | 102.9 | 103.68 | 103.8 | 103.59 | | | | |
| KOTAKNIFTY | EQ | 05-Jun-20 | 103.8 | 104.09 | 105.65 | 104.03 | 105.45 | 105.02 | 104.73 | | | | |
| KOTAKNIFTY | EQ | 08-Jun-20 | 105.02 | 106.62 | 106.8 | 105 | 105.98 | 105.29 | 106.1 | | | | |
| KOTAKNIFTY | EQ | 09-Jun-20 | 105.29 | 105.3 | 106.9 | 99 | 104 | 104.1 | 105.37 | | | | |
| KOTAKNIFTY | EQ | 10-Jun-20 | 104.1 | 104.45 | 105.61 | 104.33 | 105.6 | 104.94 | 104.93 | | | | |
| KOTAKNIFTY | EQ | 11-Jun-20 | 104.94 | 104.94 | 113.9 | 102.97 | 103.5 | 103.28 | 106.74 | | | | |
| KOTAKNIFTY | EQ | 12-Jun-20 | 103.28 | 101.98 | 103.94 | 100 | 103.75 | 103.56 | 101.72 | | | | |
| KOTAKNIFTY | EQ | 15-Jun-20 | 103.56 | 103.22 | 103.25 | 101.02 | 102.24 | 102.13 | 102.04 | | | | |
| KOTAKNIFTY | EQ | 16-Jun-20 | 102.13 | 106.2 | 108.92 | 101 | 102.65 | 102.74 | 103.1 | | | | |
| KOTAKNIFTY | EQ | 17-Jun-20 | 102.74 | 103 | 103.72 | 102.2 | 102.3 | 102.56 | 102.94 | | | | |
| KOTAKNIFTY | EQ | 18-Jun-20 | 102.56 | 102.89 | 104.9 | 102.05 | 104.16 | 104.37 | 103.7 | | | | |
| KOTAKNIFTY | EQ | 19-Jun-20 | 104.37 | 104.9 | 106.42 | 104.49 | 106.4 | 105.88 | 105.33 | | | | |
| KOTAKNIFTY | EQ | 22-Jun-20 | 105.88 | 105.88 | 107.39 | 105.88 | 106.7 | 106.59 | 106.75 | | | | |
| KOTAKNIFTY | EQ | 23-Jun-20 | 106.59 | 106.54 | 108.5 | 106.54 | 108.5 | 108.2 | 107.39 | 30 June value at close | | 106492.32 | |
| KOTAKNIFTY | EQ | 24-Jun-20 | 108.2 | 108.2 | 109.21 | 106.11 | 106.95 | 106.3 | 108.02 | Basic Value | | 106607.64 | |

| | | | | | | | | | | | | | |
|---|---|---|---|---|---|---|---|---|---|---|---|---|---|
| KOTAKNIFTY | EQ | 25-Jun-20 | 106.3 | 105.99 | 107.27 | 105.6 | 105.99 | 106.05 | 106.37 | Profit / Loss | | -115.32 | |
| KOTAKNIFTY | EQ | 26-Jun-20 | 106.05 | 106.45 | 108.07 | 106.41 | 107.99 | 107.42 | 107.16 | Profit in percentage | | -0.10817236 | |
| KOTAKNIFTY | EQ | 29-Jun-20 | 107.42 | 107.04 | 107.4 | 105.79 | 107 | 106.67 | 106.36 | 4x Adjustment % | | 0.43268944 | |
| KOTAKNIFTY | EQ | 30-Jun-20 | 106.67 | 107 | 107.86 | 106.35 | 107 | 106.92 | 107.13 | Next SIP Amount | | 10000 | |
| KOTAKNIFTY | EQ | 01-Jul-20 | 106.92 | 106.67 | 108.5 | 106 | 108.1 | 108.4 | 107.45 | 9992.85 | 93 | 116600.49 | 1089 |
| 117013.05 | | | | | | | | | | | | | |
| KOTAKNIFTY | EQ | 02-Jul-20 | 108.4 | 109 | 109.6 | 107.93 | 109.45 | 109.3 | 109.02 | | | | |
| KOTAKNIFTY | EQ | 03-Jul-20 | 109.3 | 109.39 | 110.19 | 109.39 | 109.68 | 109.9 | 109.91 | | | | |
| KOTAKNIFTY | EQ | 06-Jul-20 | 109.9 | 110.33 | 111.78 | 110.33 | 111.1 | 111.15 | 111.32 | | | | |
| KOTAKNIFTY | EQ | 07-Jul-20 | 111.15 | 112.25 | 112.32 | 110.95 | 112.28 | 111.99 | 111.19 | | | | |
| KOTAKNIFTY | EQ | 08-Jul-20 | 111.99 | 111.99 | 112.8 | 110.9 | 111.4 | 111.2 | 112.01 | | | | |
| KOTAKNIFTY | EQ | 09-Jul-20 | 111.2 | 111.29 | 112.5 | 111.29 | 112.07 | 112.06 | 111.56 | | | | |
| KOTAKNIFTY | EQ | 10-Jul-20 | 112.06 | 111.6 | 112 | 111.08 | 111.56 | 111.57 | 111.58 | | | | |
| KOTAKNIFTY | EQ | 13-Jul-20 | 111.57 | 112.2 | 112.86 | 111.5 | 112.48 | 112.55 | 112.46 | | | | |
| KOTAKNIFTY | EQ | 14-Jul-20 | 112.55 | 112.43 | 112.43 | 109.86 | 110.3 | 110.18 | 110.48 | | | | |
| KOTAKNIFTY | EQ | 15-Jul-20 | 110.18 | 110.89 | 112.17 | 109.9 | 110.5 | 110.43 | 111.56 | | | | |
| KOTAKNIFTY | EQ | 16-Jul-20 | 110.43 | 113.7 | 115.98 | 109.9 | 111.2 | 111.29 | 110.75 | | | | |
| KOTAKNIFTY | EQ | 17-Jul-20 | 111.29 | 112 | 113.1 | 111.69 | 112.99 | 112.63 | 112.43 | | | | |
| KOTAKNIFTY | EQ | 20-Jul-20 | 112.63 | 113 | 114.4 | 113 | 114.38 | 114.29 | 113.71 | | | | |
| KOTAKNIFTY | EQ | 21-Jul-20 | 114.29 | 114.2 | 116.25 | 114.2 | 115.65 | 116.03 | 115.34 | | | | |
| KOTAKNIFTY | EQ | 22-Jul-20 | 116.03 | 115.95 | 116.24 | 114.61 | 115.55 | 115.29 | 115.68 | | | | |
| KOTAKNIFTY | EQ | 23-Jul-20 | 115.29 | 115.95 | 116.46 | 115.66 | 116.34 | 116.16 | 116.17 | | | | |
| KOTAKNIFTY | EQ | 24-Jul-20 | 116.16 | 116.16 | 119.4 | 111.35 | 116.45 | 115.96 | 115.72 | 31 Jul 20 value at close | | 125616.15 | |
| KOTAKNIFTY | EQ | 27-Jul-20 | 115.96 | 133.4 | 133.4 | 114.9 | 115.22 | 115.31 | 115.38 | Basic Value | | 116600.49 | |
| KOTAKNIFTY | EQ | 28-Jul-20 | 115.31 | 115 | 117.51 | 111 | 117 | 117.27 | 116.76 | Profit / Loss | | 9015.66 | |
| KOTAKNIFTY | EQ | 29-Jul-20 | 117.27 | 117.2 | 117.68 | 115.99 | 116.27 | 116.22 | 116.85 | Profit in percentage | | 7.732094436 | |
| KOTAKNIFTY | EQ | 30-Jul-20 | 116.22 | 117 | 117.2 | 115.05 | 115.07 | 115.35 | 116.67 | 4x Adjustment % | | -23.19628331 | |
| KOTAKNIFTY | EQ | 31-Jul-20 | 115.35 | 115.7 | 115.88 | 115 | 115.5 | 115.35 | 115.43 | Next SIP Amount | | 7600 | |
| KOTAKNIFTY | EQ | 03-Aug-20 | 115.35 | 115.87 | 115.87 | 113.22 | 113.35 | 113.41 | 113.87 | 7629.29 | 67 | 124229.78 | 1156 |
| 131633.72 | | | | | | | | | | | | | |
| KOTAKNIFTY | EQ | 04-Aug-20 | 113.41 | 114 | 115.65 | 113.5 | 115.06 | 115.38 | 114.87 | | | | |
| KOTAKNIFTY | EQ | 05-Aug-20 | 115.38 | 115.9 | 116.5 | 115.15 | 116 | 115.72 | 115.94 | | | | |
| KOTAKNIFTY | EQ | 06-Aug-20 | 115.72 | 116 | 116.8 | 115.41 | 116.3 | 116.06 | 116.02 | | | | |
| KOTAKNIFTY | EQ | 07-Aug-20 | 116.06 | 116.01 | 116.73 | 115.82 | 116.5 | 116.55 | 116.27 | | | | |

| | | | | | | | | | | | |
|---|---|---|---|---|---|---|---|---|---|---|---|
| KOTAKNIFTY | EQ | 10-Aug-20 | 116.55 | 116.61 | 117.5 | 116.61 | 117.25 | 116.97 | 117.13 | | |
| KOTAKNIFTY | EQ | 11-Aug-20 | 116.97 | 119 | 119 | 117.29 | 118 | 117.98 | 117.81 | | |
| KOTAKNIFTY | EQ | 12-Aug-20 | 117.98 | 118 | 118 | 116.32 | 117.68 | 117.48 | 117.15 | | |
| KOTAKNIFTY | EQ | 13-Aug-20 | 117.48 | 117.86 | 118.02 | 117.26 | 117.4 | 117.4 | 117.59 | | |
| KOTAKNIFTY | EQ | 14-Aug-20 | 117.4 | 117.56 | 118.25 | 115.8 | 116.7 | 116.31 | 117.44 | | |
| KOTAKNIFTY | EQ | 17-Aug-20 | 116.31 | 116.31 | 117.5 | 116 | 117 | 116.76 | 116.58 | | |
| KOTAKNIFTY | EQ | 18-Aug-20 | 116.76 | 117 | 118.44 | 117 | 118.4 | 118.13 | 117.83 | | |
| KOTAKNIFTY | EQ | 19-Aug-20 | 118.13 | 118.5 | 119.3 | 118.5 | 118.8 | 118.9 | 118.95 | | |
| KOTAKNIFTY | EQ | 20-Aug-20 | 118.9 | 118.9 | 118.9 | 117.21 | 117.8 | 117.81 | 117.79 | | |
| KOTAKNIFTY | EQ | 21-Aug-20 | 117.81 | 118.8 | 119 | 117.97 | 118.1 | 118.1 | 118.38 | | |
| KOTAKNIFTY | EQ | 24-Aug-20 | 118.1 | 119.08 | 119.25 | 118.41 | 119 | 118.99 | 118.86 | | |
| KOTAKNIFTY | EQ | 25-Aug-20 | 118.99 | 119.25 | 119.58 | 118.79 | 119.22 | 119.12 | 119.32 | 28 Aug 20 value at close | 139725.72 |
| KOTAKNIFTY | EQ | 26-Aug-20 | 119.12 | 119.55 | 120 | 119.02 | 119.99 | 119.98 | 119.39 | Basic Value | 124229.78 |
| KOTAKNIFTY | EQ | 27-Aug-20 | 119.98 | 120.04 | 120.6 | 120.01 | 120.1 | 120.1 | 120.31 | Profit / Loss | 15495.94 |
| KOTAKNIFTY | EQ | 28-Aug-20 | 120.1 | 120.33 | 121.14 | 120.33 | 121 | 120.87 | 120.83 | Profit in percentage | 12.4736114 |

# APPENDIX-F

| Symbol | Series | Date | Prev Close | Open Price | High Price | Low Price | Last Price | Close Price | Average Price | Investment | share buy at average price | total investment | Total Share | Value at Close |
|---|---|---|---|---|---|---|---|---|---|---|---|---|---|---|
| KOTAKNIFTY | EQ | 30-Aug-19 | 113.98 | 113.95 | 114.4 | 112.75 | 113.71 | 113.58 | 113.28 | | | | | |
| KOTAKNIFTY | EQ | 03-Sep-19 | 113.58 | 111.3 | 113.42 | 111 | 111.89 | 111.82 | 112.54 | 10016.06 | 89 | 10016.06 | 89 | 9951.98 |
| KOTAKNIFTY | EQ | 04-Sep-19 | 111.82 | 112 | 112.81 | 111.68 | 112.6 | 112.5 | 112.14 | | | | | |
| KOTAKNIFTY | EQ | 05-Sep-19 | 112.5 | 112.81 | 113.3 | 111.98 | 112.25 | 112.41 | 112.69 | | | | | |
| KOTAKNIFTY | EQ | 06-Sep-19 | 112.41 | 112.5 | 113.35 | 112.1 | 112.9 | 112.9 | 112.89 | | | | | |
| KOTAKNIFTY | EQ | 09-Sep-19 | 112.9 | 113 | 114.19 | 112.4 | 113.3 | 113.52 | 113.59 | | | | | |
| KOTAKNIFTY | EQ | 11-Sep-19 | 113.52 | 114.05 | 114.45 | 113.5 | 114.24 | 114.22 | 114.02 | | | | | |
| KOTAKNIFTY | EQ | 12-Sep-19 | 114.22 | 114 | 114.9 | 113.7 | 113.7 | 113.72 | 114.51 | | | | | |
| KOTAKNIFTY | EQ | 13-Sep-19 | 113.72 | 113.72 | 114.5 | 113.05 | 114.35 | 114.33 | 113.63 | | | | | |
| KOTAKNIFTY | EQ | 16-Sep-19 | 114.33 | 114.27 | 114.49 | 113.46 | 113.75 | 113.95 | 113.99 | | | | | |
| KOTAKNIFTY | EQ | 17-Sep-19 | 113.95 | 113.5 | 113.86 | 111.85 | 111.9 | 112.15 | 112.77 | | | | | |
| KOTAKNIFTY | EQ | 18-Sep-19 | 112.15 | 112.7 | 112.85 | 111.9 | 112.67 | 112.26 | 112.34 | | | | | |
| KOTAKNIFTY | EQ | 19-Sep-19 | 112.26 | 112.35 | 112.4 | 110.94 | 111.1 | 111.07 | 111.2 | | | | | |
| KOTAKNIFTY | EQ | 20-Sep-19 | 111.07 | 113 | 117.4 | 110.8 | 116.5 | 116.37 | 115.08 | | | | | |
| KOTAKNIFTY | EQ | 23-Sep-19 | 116.37 | 120 | 125 | 118 | 121.5 | 120.59 | 121.62 | | | | | |
| KOTAKNIFTY | EQ | 24-Sep-19 | 120.59 | 120.59 | 123 | 119.31 | 119.8 | 119.93 | 121.28 | | | | | |
| KOTAKNIFTY | EQ | 25-Sep-19 | 119.93 | 118.55 | 119.95 | 118.55 | 118.8 | 118.88 | 119 | | | | | |
| KOTAKNIFTY | EQ | 26-Sep-19 | 118.88 | 119.2 | 120.25 | 119.2 | 119.6 | 119.62 | 119.51 | | | | | |
| KOTAKNIFTY | EQ | 27-Sep-19 | 119.62 | 120 | 120.15 | 119.3 | 119.3 | 119.52 | 119.8 | | | | | |
| KOTAKNIFTY | EQ | 30-Sep-19 | 119.52 | 119.56 | 119.7 | 118.23 | 119.65 | 119.46 | 119.29 | | | | | |
| KOTAKNIFTY | EQ | 01-Oct-19 | 119.46 | 119.51 | 120 | 117 | 117.6 | 117.49 | 118.77 | 9976.68 | 84 | 19992.74 | 173 | 20325.77 |
| KOTAKNIFTY | EQ | 03-Oct-19 | 117.49 | 117.01 | 117.79 | 116.5 | 117.2 | 117.08 | 117.13 | | | | | |
| KOTAKNIFTY | EQ | 04-Oct-19 | 117.08 | 117.4 | 117.9 | 115.95 | 116.04 | 116.03 | 116.96 | | | | | |
| KOTAKNIFTY | EQ | 07-Oct-19 | 116.03 | 116.15 | 116.7 | 115.36 | 115.65 | 115.82 | 116.33 | | | | | |
| KOTAKNIFTY | EQ | 09-Oct-19 | 115.82 | 118.1 | 128.6 | 115.25 | 117.39 | 116.97 | 115.91 | | | | | |
| KOTAKNIFTY | EQ | 10-Oct-19 | 116.97 | 116.82 | 117.08 | 116.06 | 116.51 | 116.45 | 116.43 | | | | | |
| KOTAKNIFTY | EQ | 11-Oct-19 | 116.45 | 116.69 | 117.47 | 115.81 | 116.98 | 116.7 | 116.64 | | | | | |
| KOTAKNIFTY | EQ | 14-Oct-19 | 116.7 | 117 | 117.9 | 116.8 | 117.6 | 117.31 | 117.31 | | | | | |
| KOTAKNIFTY | EQ | 15-Oct-19 | 117.31 | 117.6 | 118.4 | 117.3 | 117.91 | 118 | 117.61 | | | | | |
| KOTAKNIFTY | EQ | 16-Oct-19 | 118 | 115.6 | 118.7 | 105 | 118.5 | 118.18 | 118.31 | | | | | |
| KOTAKNIFTY | EQ | 17-Oct-19 | 118.18 | 118.02 | 119.64 | 118.02 | 119.64 | 119.49 | 118.88 | | | | | |
| KOTAKNIFTY | EQ | 18-Oct-19 | 119.49 | 118.95 | 121 | 118.95 | 120.55 | 120.36 | 120.36 | | | | | |

| | | | | | | | | | | | | | | |
|---|---|---|---|---|---|---|---|---|---|---|---|---|---|---|
| KOTAKNIFTY | EQ | 22-Oct-19 | 120.36 | 120.61 | 121 | 119.75 | 120.25 | 119.98 | 120.36 | | | | | |
| KOTAKNIFTY | EQ | 23-Oct-19 | 119.98 | 120 | 120.5 | 119.5 | 119.51 | 119.6 | 119.86 | | | | | |
| KOTAKNIFTY | EQ | 24-Oct-19 | 119.6 | 120.06 | 120.78 | 119.5 | 120 | 119.91 | 120.23 | | | | | |
| KOTAKNIFTY | EQ | 25-Oct-19 | 119.91 | 119.99 | 120.6 | 119.5 | 120.5 | 120.34 | 119.7 | | | | | |
| KOTAKNIFTY | EQ | 27-Oct-19 | 120.34 | 121.11 | 121.11 | 119.91 | 120.6 | 120.29 | 120.25 | | | | | |
| KOTAKNIFTY | EQ | 29-Oct-19 | 120.29 | 120.16 | 122 | 120.12 | 121.54 | 121.74 | 121.55 | | | | | |
| KOTAKNIFTY | EQ | 30-Oct-19 | 121.74 | 121.7 | 122.68 | 121.7 | 122 | 122.12 | 122.15 | | | | | |
| KOTAKNIFTY | EQ | 31-Oct-19 | 122.12 | 122.39 | 123.2 | 122.2 | 122.33 | 122.52 | 122.7 | | | | | |
| KOTAKNIFTY | EQ | 01-Nov-19 | 122.52 | 122.5 | 123.68 | 122.26 | 122.8 | 122.84 | 122.82 | 9948.42 | 81 | 29941.16 | 254 | 31201.36 |
| KOTAKNIFTY | EQ | 04-Nov-19 | 122.84 | 123.17 | 123.89 | 122.49 | 123.45 | 123.28 | 123.27 | | | | | |
| KOTAKNIFTY | EQ | 05-Nov-19 | 123.28 | 123.1 | 123.55 | 122.6 | 123.25 | 123.22 | 123.23 | | | | | |
| KOTAKNIFTY | EQ | 06-Nov-19 | 123.22 | 123 | 124 | 122.56 | 123.46 | 123.59 | 123.54 | | | | | |
| KOTAKNIFTY | EQ | 07-Nov-19 | 123.59 | 123.6 | 124.3 | 123.5 | 124.11 | 124 | 123.88 | | | | | |
| KOTAKNIFTY | EQ | 08-Nov-19 | 124 | 123.8 | 124.65 | 123 | 123.2 | 123.27 | 123.69 | | | | | |
| KOTAKNIFTY | EQ | 11-Nov-19 | 123.27 | 123.11 | 123.72 | 122.47 | 123.09 | 123.19 | 123.08 | | | | | |
| KOTAKNIFTY | EQ | 13-Nov-19 | 123.19 | 123.39 | 123.55 | 122.17 | 122.68 | 122.34 | 122.94 | | | | | |
| KOTAKNIFTY | EQ | 14-Nov-19 | 122.34 | 122.68 | 123 | 121.9 | 122.5 | 122.48 | 122.49 | | | | | |
| KOTAKNIFTY | EQ | 15-Nov-19 | 122.48 | 124.9 | 125 | 122.52 | 123.07 | 123.09 | 123.01 | | | | | |
| KOTAKNIFTY | EQ | 18-Nov-19 | 123.09 | 123.31 | 123.32 | 122.74 | 122.9 | 122.77 | 122.95 | | | | | |
| KOTAKNIFTY | EQ | 19-Nov-19 | 122.77 | 123.3 | 123.5 | 122.55 | 123.5 | 123.36 | 123.17 | | | | | |
| KOTAKNIFTY | EQ | 20-Nov-19 | 123.36 | 120.9 | 125.8 | 109.8 | 123.6 | 123.78 | 123.91 | | | | | |
| KOTAKNIFTY | EQ | 21-Nov-19 | 123.78 | 124 | 124.4 | 122.15 | 124.01 | 123.9 | 123.82 | | | | | |
| KOTAKNIFTY | EQ | 22-Nov-19 | 123.9 | 123.9 | 123.9 | 122.9 | 123.43 | 122.99 | 123.44 | | | | | |
| KOTAKNIFTY | EQ | 25-Nov-19 | 122.99 | 123.23 | 124.62 | 122.92 | 124.56 | 124.57 | 124.34 | | | | | |
| KOTAKNIFTY | EQ | 26-Nov-19 | 124.57 | 124.65 | 124.95 | 124.04 | 124.59 | 124.74 | 124.78 | | | | | |
| KOTAKNIFTY | EQ | 27-Nov-19 | 124.74 | 124.62 | 124.97 | 124.6 | 124.75 | 124.86 | 124.82 | | | | | |
| KOTAKNIFTY | EQ | 28-Nov-19 | 124.86 | 124.74 | 126.45 | 124.74 | 126.32 | 126.3 | 125.88 | | | | | |
| KOTAKNIFTY | EQ | 29-Nov-19 | 126.3 | 126.22 | 126.22 | 124.8 | 125.45 | 125.34 | 125.29 | | | | | |
| KOTAKNIFTY | EQ | 02-Dec-19 | 125.34 | 124.81 | 125.56 | 123.75 | 125.08 | 125.01 | 125.02 | 10001.6 | 80 | 39942.76 | 334 | 41753.34 |
| KOTAKNIFTY | EQ | 03-Dec-19 | 125.01 | 125.05 | 125.05 | 123.67 | 124.25 | 124.19 | 124.26 | | | | | |
| KOTAKNIFTY | EQ | 04-Dec-19 | 124.19 | 126.7 | 129.2 | 123.7 | 125.03 | 124.75 | 124.31 | | | | | |
| KOTAKNIFTY | EQ | 05-Dec-19 | 124.75 | 125.99 | 125.99 | 124.02 | 124.18 | 124.28 | 124.59 | | | | | |
| KOTAKNIFTY | EQ | 06-Dec-19 | 124.28 | 124.77 | 124.8 | 123.65 | 123.95 | 124.25 | 124.24 | | | | | |
| KOTAKNIFTY | EQ | 09-Dec-19 | 124.25 | 126.7 | 129.2 | 123.5 | 123.95 | 123.94 | 123.92 | | | | | |

| | | | | | | | | | | | | | | |
|---|---|---|---|---|---|---|---|---|---|---|---|---|---|---|
| KOTAKNIFTY | EQ | 10-Dec-19 | 123.94 | 125.9 | 125.9 | 122.58 | 123.45 | 123.21 | 123.19 | | | | | |
| KOTAKNIFTY | EQ | 11-Dec-19 | 123.21 | 124 | 124 | 122.8 | 123.2 | 123.11 | 123.2 | | | | | |
| KOTAKNIFTY | EQ | 12-Dec-19 | 123.11 | 123.11 | 124.57 | 123.11 | 123.94 | 123.95 | 123.96 | | | | | |
| KOTAKNIFTY | EQ | 13-Dec-19 | 123.95 | 124.24 | 125.45 | 124.21 | 125.4 | 125.12 | 124.78 | | | | | |
| KOTAKNIFTY | EQ | 16-Dec-19 | 125.12 | 125 | 125.48 | 124.6 | 124.75 | 124.77 | 125.01 | | | | | |
| KOTAKNIFTY | EQ | 17-Dec-19 | 124.77 | 124.8 | 125.86 | 124.8 | 125.83 | 125.73 | 125.44 | | | | | |
| KOTAKNIFTY | EQ | 18-Dec-19 | 125.73 | 125.95 | 126.3 | 125.56 | 126.3 | 126.15 | 125.93 | | | | | |
| KOTAKNIFTY | EQ | 19-Dec-19 | 126.15 | 126.35 | 126.5 | 125.72 | 126.5 | 126.39 | 126.18 | | | | | |
| KOTAKNIFTY | EQ | 20-Dec-19 | 126.39 | 126.39 | 126.78 | 126.39 | 126.4 | 126.49 | 126.51 | | | | | |
| KOTAKNIFTY | EQ | 23-Dec-19 | 126.49 | 140.4 | 149.3 | 126.1 | 126.6 | 126.44 | 126.47 | | | | | |
| KOTAKNIFTY | EQ | 24-Dec-19 | 126.44 | 126.4 | 126.97 | 126.1 | 126.45 | 126.37 | 126.6 | | | | | |
| KOTAKNIFTY | EQ | 26-Dec-19 | 126.37 | 127.39 | 127.39 | 125.05 | 125.52 | 125.4 | 125.71 | | | | | |
| KOTAKNIFTY | EQ | 27-Dec-19 | 125.4 | 125.5 | 127 | 125.2 | 126.54 | 126.56 | 126.01 | | | | | |
| KOTAKNIFTY | EQ | 30-Dec-19 | 126.56 | 129.1 | 130 | 126.49 | 127.25 | 127.46 | 127.33 | | | | | |
| KOTAKNIFTY | EQ | 31-Dec-19 | 127.46 | 126.6 | 127.46 | 126.25 | 126.95 | 126.82 | 126.74 | | | | | |
| KOTAKNIFTY | EQ | 01-Jan-20 | 126.82 | 127.79 | 130 | 125.89 | 126.35 | 126.47 | 126.49 | 9992.71 | 79 | | 49935.47 | 413 | 52232.11 |
| KOTAKNIFTY | EQ | 02-Jan-20 | 126.47 | 135.3 | 135.3 | 126.41 | 127.2 | 127.01 | 126.91 | | | | | |
| KOTAKNIFTY | EQ | 03-Jan-20 | 127.01 | 127.01 | 132.46 | 126.14 | 126.44 | 126.33 | 128.39 | | | | | |
| KOTAKNIFTY | EQ | 06-Jan-20 | 126.33 | 126 | 126.38 | 124.45 | 124.7 | 124.65 | 125.28 | | | | | |
| KOTAKNIFTY | EQ | 07-Jan-20 | 124.65 | 124.71 | 126.3 | 124.71 | 125.2 | 125.24 | 125.48 | | | | | |
| KOTAKNIFTY | EQ | 08-Jan-20 | 125.24 | 125.24 | 125.24 | 123.91 | 124.65 | 124.82 | 124.38 | | | | | |
| KOTAKNIFTY | EQ | 09-Jan-20 | 124.82 | 125.59 | 126.74 | 125.55 | 126.45 | 126.47 | 126.42 | | | | | |
| KOTAKNIFTY | EQ | 10-Jan-20 | 126.47 | 127.05 | 127.5 | 126.45 | 126.7 | 126.72 | 127.21 | | | | | |
| KOTAKNIFTY | EQ | 13-Jan-20 | 126.72 | 127.14 | 127.69 | 127.14 | 127.64 | 127.5 | 127.45 | | | | | |
| KOTAKNIFTY | EQ | 14-Jan-20 | 127.5 | 128.5 | 128.5 | 127.28 | 127.87 | 127.87 | 127.63 | | | | | |
| KOTAKNIFTY | EQ | 15-Jan-20 | 127.87 | 127.7 | 128 | 127.2 | 128 | 127.98 | 127.63 | | | | | |
| KOTAKNIFTY | EQ | 16-Jan-20 | 127.98 | 136.9 | 139.5 | 116.5 | 127.8 | 127.84 | 128.11 | | | | | |
| KOTAKNIFTY | EQ | 17-Jan-20 | 127.84 | 127.84 | 128.34 | 127.48 | 127.81 | 128.09 | 128.04 | | | | | |
| KOTAKNIFTY | EQ | 20-Jan-20 | 128.09 | 128.09 | 128.09 | 126.91 | 127.24 | 127.02 | 127.44 | | | | | |
| KOTAKNIFTY | EQ | 21-Jan-20 | 127.02 | 127.02 | 127.07 | 126.05 | 126.2 | 126.25 | 126.61 | | | | | |
| KOTAKNIFTY | EQ | 22-Jan-20 | 126.25 | 126.95 | 126.95 | 125.5 | 125.86 | 125.74 | 126.07 | | | | | |
| KOTAKNIFTY | EQ | 23-Jan-20 | 125.74 | 125.95 | 126.61 | 125.4 | 126.5 | 126.35 | 126.26 | | | | | |
| KOTAKNIFTY | EQ | 24-Jan-20 | 126.35 | 126.07 | 127.4 | 125.79 | 127.4 | 127.33 | 127.18 | | | | | |
| KOTAKNIFTY | EQ | 27-Jan-20 | 127.33 | 126.53 | 126.95 | 125.65 | 126.2 | 126.09 | 126.36 | | | | | |

| | | | | | | | | | | | | | | |
|---|---|---|---|---|---|---|---|---|---|---|---|---|---|---|
| KOTAKNIFTY | EQ | 28-Jan-20 | 126.09 | 127.38 | 127.38 | 125 | 125.53 | 125.27 | 125.52 | | | | | |
| KOTAKNIFTY | EQ | 29-Jan-20 | 125.27 | 125.9 | 126.29 | 125.02 | 125.89 | 125.68 | 125.7 | | | | | |
| KOTAKNIFTY | EQ | 30-Jan-20 | 125.68 | 125.4 | 125.65 | 124.6 | 125.25 | 125.36 | 125.22 | | | | | |
| KOTAKNIFTY | EQ | 31-Jan-20 | 125.36 | 125.5 | 125.54 | 123.99 | 124.21 | 124 | 124.5 | | | | | |
| KOTAKNIFTY | EQ | 01-Feb-20 | 124 | 123.81 | 125 | 122.31 | 122.6 | 122.77 | 124.32 | 9945.6 | 80 | 59881.07 | 493 | 60525.61 |
| KOTAKNIFTY | EQ | 03-Feb-20 | 122.77 | 121.64 | 122.18 | 121.1 | 121.7 | 121.33 | 121.7 | | | | | |
| KOTAKNIFTY | EQ | 04-Feb-20 | 121.33 | 123.48 | 124.5 | 122 | 124.4 | 124.38 | 124.03 | | | | | |
| KOTAKNIFTY | EQ | 05-Feb-20 | 124.38 | 124.4 | 125.5 | 124 | 125.5 | 125.25 | 124.82 | | | | | |
| KOTAKNIFTY | EQ | 06-Feb-20 | 125.25 | 125.31 | 125.95 | 125.14 | 125.5 | 125.6 | 125.51 | | | | | |
| KOTAKNIFTY | EQ | 07-Feb-20 | 125.6 | 125.12 | 125.95 | 125.01 | 125.45 | 125.44 | 125.43 | | | | | |
| KOTAKNIFTY | EQ | 10-Feb-20 | 125.44 | 125.44 | 125.44 | 124.16 | 124.95 | 124.69 | 124.72 | | | | | |
| KOTAKNIFTY | EQ | 11-Feb-20 | 124.69 | 124.89 | 126.15 | 124.89 | 125.45 | 125.48 | 125.55 | | | | | |
| KOTAKNIFTY | EQ | 12-Feb-20 | 125.48 | 126 | 128.7 | 125.9 | 126.55 | 126.6 | 127.77 | | | | | |
| KOTAKNIFTY | EQ | 13-Feb-20 | 126.6 | 126.55 | 126.55 | 125.72 | 126.25 | 126.01 | 125.91 | | | | | |
| KOTAKNIFTY | EQ | 14-Feb-20 | 126.01 | 126.9 | 126.9 | 125.1 | 125.49 | 125.29 | 126.09 | | | | | |
| KOTAKNIFTY | EQ | 17-Feb-20 | 125.29 | 131.8 | 131.8 | 124.73 | 125.28 | 125.2 | 125.24 | | | | | |
| KOTAKNIFTY | EQ | 18-Feb-20 | 125.2 | 124.7 | 124.79 | 123.77 | 124.63 | 124.41 | 124.24 | | | | | |
| KOTAKNIFTY | EQ | 19-Feb-20 | 124.41 | 125.35 | 125.74 | 124.76 | 125.72 | 125.69 | 125.07 | | | | | |
| KOTAKNIFTY | EQ | 20-Feb-20 | 125.69 | 125.69 | 125.75 | 125.04 | 125.5 | 125.44 | 125.62 | | | | | |
| KOTAKNIFTY | EQ | 24-Feb-20 | 125.44 | 127.9 | 130.5 | 122.75 | 123.4 | 123.09 | 123.71 | | | | | |
| KOTAKNIFTY | EQ | 25-Feb-20 | 123.09 | 123.1 | 123.5 | 122.48 | 122.75 | 122.56 | 123.04 | | | | | |
| KOTAKNIFTY | EQ | 26-Feb-20 | 122.56 | 122 | 122.3 | 120.77 | 121.68 | 121.39 | 121.63 | | | | | |
| KOTAKNIFTY | EQ | 27-Feb-20 | 121.39 | 121.2 | 121.2 | 120.15 | 120.74 | 120.55 | 120.51 | | | | | |
| KOTAKNIFTY | EQ | 28-Feb-20 | 120.55 | 119.5 | 119.5 | 116.15 | 118 | 116.78 | 117.53 | | | | | |
| KOTAKNIFTY | EQ | 02-Mar-20 | 116.78 | 118.28 | 118.59 | 116.23 | 116.72 | 116.79 | 117.6 | 9996 | 85 | 69877.07 | 578 | 67504.62 |
| KOTAKNIFTY | EQ | 03-Mar-20 | 116.79 | 119.1 | 121.5 | 116.15 | 117.45 | 117.43 | 116.95 | | | | | |
| KOTAKNIFTY | EQ | 04-Mar-20 | 117.43 | 117.34 | 117.78 | 115.5 | 117 | 116.87 | 116.56 | | | | | |
| KOTAKNIFTY | EQ | 05-Mar-20 | 116.87 | 119.2 | 119.2 | 116.93 | 117.02 | 117.13 | 117.37 | | | | | |
| KOTAKNIFTY | EQ | 06-Mar-20 | 117.13 | 119.5 | 121.8 | 112.6 | 114.2 | 114.83 | 114.47 | | | | | |
| KOTAKNIFTY | EQ | 09-Mar-20 | 114.83 | 117.1 | 119.4 | 108.1 | 109 | 109.95 | 110.04 | | | | | |
| KOTAKNIFTY | EQ | 11-Mar-20 | 109.95 | 109.95 | 109.95 | 107.96 | 109.11 | 109.16 | 108.89 | | | | | |
| KOTAKNIFTY | EQ | 12-Mar-20 | 109.16 | 109.16 | 109.16 | 100.2 | 102 | 101.83 | 103.38 | | | | | |
| KOTAKNIFTY | EQ | 13-Mar-20 | 101.83 | 110 | 110 | 93.1 | 105.1 | 104.73 | 100.07 | | | | | |
| KOTAKNIFTY | EQ | 16-Mar-20 | 104.73 | 104.73 | 104.73 | 95.9 | 96.35 | 96.58 | 98.6 | | | | | |

| | | | | | | | | | | | | | | |
|---|---|---|---|---|---|---|---|---|---|---|---|---|---|---|
| KOTAKNIFTY | EQ | 17-Mar-20 | 96.58 | 123.96 | 123.96 | 94 | 96.8 | 95.29 | 96.63 | | | | | |
| KOTAKNIFTY | EQ | 18-Mar-20 | 95.29 | 97 | 97 | 89.95 | 90 | 90.45 | 91.85 | | | | | |
| KOTAKNIFTY | EQ | 19-Mar-20 | 90.45 | 90.45 | 91.97 | 85.15 | 86.5 | 86.26 | 87.19 | | | | | |
| KOTAKNIFTY | EQ | 20-Mar-20 | 86.26 | 88.49 | 91.41 | 85.25 | 90 | 89.96 | 89.42 | | | | | |
| KOTAKNIFTY | EQ | 23-Mar-20 | 89.96 | 85 | 87 | 81.01 | 83 | 82.09 | 82.71 | | | | | |
| KOTAKNIFTY | EQ | 24-Mar-20 | 82.09 | 88 | 101 | 81.95 | 84.4 | 84.04 | 84.42 | | | | | |
| KOTAKNIFTY | EQ | 25-Mar-20 | 84.04 | 84.1 | 87 | 82.2 | 85.8 | 86.22 | 84.7 | | | | | |
| KOTAKNIFTY | EQ | 26-Mar-20 | 86.22 | 86.22 | 90.9 | 85.5 | 88.99 | 89.39 | 89.19 | | | | | |
| KOTAKNIFTY | EQ | 27-Mar-20 | 89.39 | 89.4 | 94.5 | 88.5 | 89.6 | 90.01 | 91.25 | | | | | |
| KOTAKNIFTY | EQ | 30-Mar-20 | 90.01 | 88.2 | 89 | 86.15 | 86.5 | 86.62 | 87.52 | | | | | |
| KOTAKNIFTY | EQ | 31-Mar-20 | 86.62 | 87.99 | 89.75 | 87 | 88.4 | 88.53 | 88.5 | | | | | |
| KOTAKNIFTY | EQ | 01-Apr-20 | 88.53 | 88.5 | 90 | 86.2 | 86.7 | 86.72 | 87.13 | 10019.95 | 115 | 79897.02 | 693 | 60096.96 |
| KOTAKNIFTY | EQ | 03-Apr-20 | 86.72 | 86.72 | 87.44 | 84 | 84.71 | 84.58 | 84.77 | | | | | |
| KOTAKNIFTY | EQ | 07-Apr-20 | 84.58 | 87.99 | 90.95 | 86 | 90.8 | 90.66 | 88.58 | | | | | |
| KOTAKNIFTY | EQ | 08-Apr-20 | 90.66 | 90.5 | 94.38 | 88.81 | 91.18 | 91.02 | 91.84 | | | | | |
| KOTAKNIFTY | EQ | 09-Apr-20 | 91.02 | 93.8 | 94.2 | 91.5 | 93.99 | 93.58 | 93.27 | | | | | |
| KOTAKNIFTY | EQ | 13-Apr-20 | 93.58 | 93.99 | 94.25 | 92.13 | 93.65 | 93.67 | 93.41 | | | | | |
| KOTAKNIFTY | EQ | 15-Apr-20 | 93.67 | 95.49 | 96 | 92.5 | 93.2 | 93.23 | 94.99 | | | | | |
| KOTAKNIFTY | EQ | 16-Apr-20 | 93.23 | 92.94 | 94.24 | 91.71 | 93.85 | 93.85 | 93.61 | | | | | |
| KOTAKNIFTY | EQ | 17-Apr-20 | 93.85 | 97.6 | 97.6 | 93.67 | 95.75 | 95.21 | 95.49 | | | | | |
| KOTAKNIFTY | EQ | 20-Apr-20 | 95.21 | 96.59 | 96.65 | 95.35 | 96.1 | 96.12 | 96.13 | | | | | |
| KOTAKNIFTY | EQ | 21-Apr-20 | 96.12 | 96 | 96 | 92.88 | 93.2 | 93.39 | 93.81 | | | | | |
| KOTAKNIFTY | EQ | 22-Apr-20 | 93.39 | 93.4 | 95.45 | 92.8 | 94.9 | 95.05 | 94.61 | | | | | |
| KOTAKNIFTY | EQ | 23-Apr-20 | 95.05 | 95.45 | 96.95 | 94.8 | 96.07 | 96.31 | 96.19 | | | | | |
| KOTAKNIFTY | EQ | 24-Apr-20 | 96.31 | 96.5 | 96.5 | 94.72 | 95.24 | 94.98 | 95.23 | | | | | |
| KOTAKNIFTY | EQ | 27-Apr-20 | 94.98 | 96.1 | 96.98 | 95.86 | 96.5 | 96.42 | 96.58 | | | | | |
| KOTAKNIFTY | EQ | 28-Apr-20 | 96.42 | 97 | 97.39 | 95.95 | 97.02 | 96.91 | 96.2 | | | | | |
| KOTAKNIFTY | EQ | 29-Apr-20 | 96.91 | 97.61 | 99.6 | 97.06 | 99.11 | 99.24 | 98.51 | | | | | |
| KOTAKNIFTY | EQ | 30-Apr-20 | 99.24 | 103.2 | 108.2 | 99.5 | 101.21 | 101.38 | 101.42 | | | | | |
| KOTAKNIFTY | EQ | 04-May-20 | 101.38 | 98.88 | 98.88 | 96 | 96.68 | 96.56 | 96.95 | 9985.85 | 103 | 89882.87 | 796 | 76861.76 |
| KOTAKNIFTY | EQ | 05-May-20 | 96.56 | 99.5 | 102.4 | 95.5 | 96 | 95.78 | 96.79 | | | | | |
| KOTAKNIFTY | EQ | 06-May-20 | 95.78 | 95.78 | 96.75 | 94.75 | 96.2 | 95.9 | 95.97 | | | | | |
| KOTAKNIFTY | EQ | 07-May-20 | 95.9 | 95.3 | 96 | 94.67 | 95.68 | 95.41 | 95.31 | | | | | |
| KOTAKNIFTY | EQ | 08-May-20 | 95.41 | 96.7 | 97.02 | 95.59 | 96.13 | 95.91 | 96.36 | | | | | |

| | | | | | | | | | | | | | | |
|---|---|---|---|---|---|---|---|---|---|---|---|---|---|---|
| KOTAKNIFTY | EQ | 11-May-20 | 95.91 | 95.91 | 97.75 | 95.5 | 95.88 | 95.77 | 96.89 | | | | | |
| KOTAKNIFTY | EQ | 12-May-20 | 95.77 | 95.3 | 96.1 | 94 | 95.92 | 95.62 | 94.8 | | | | | |
| KOTAKNIFTY | EQ | 13-May-20 | 95.62 | 99 | 99.41 | 97.21 | 97.25 | 97.5 | 97.91 | | | | | |
| KOTAKNIFTY | EQ | 14-May-20 | 97.5 | 96.6 | 96.6 | 95.06 | 95.65 | 95.58 | 95.69 | | | | | |
| KOTAKNIFTY | EQ | 15-May-20 | 95.58 | 96 | 96 | 94 | 94.93 | 94.96 | 94.49 | | | | | |
| KOTAKNIFTY | EQ | 18-May-20 | 94.96 | 95 | 95 | 91.73 | 92.28 | 91.9 | 92.47 | | | | | |
| KOTAKNIFTY | EQ | 19-May-20 | 91.9 | 93 | 93.96 | 92.2 | 92.51 | 92.58 | 92.92 | | | | | |
| KOTAKNIFTY | EQ | 20-May-20 | 92.58 | 92.58 | 94.6 | 92.5 | 94.6 | 94.15 | 93.31 | | | | | |
| KOTAKNIFTY | EQ | 21-May-20 | 94.15 | 94.45 | 95.15 | 94.05 | 94.57 | 94.56 | 94.6 | | | | | |
| KOTAKNIFTY | EQ | 22-May-20 | 94.56 | 94.01 | 95 | 93.5 | 94.09 | 93.86 | 93.92 | | | | | |
| KOTAKNIFTY | EQ | 26-May-20 | 93.86 | 94.9 | 95.2 | 93.7 | 93.99 | 94.08 | 94.5 | | | | | |
| KOTAKNIFTY | EQ | 27-May-20 | 94.08 | 94.9 | 96.5 | 93.7 | 96.4 | 96.22 | 95.23 | | | | | |
| KOTAKNIFTY | EQ | 28-May-20 | 96.22 | 96 | 98 | 96 | 97.8 | 97.85 | 97.45 | | | | | |
| KOTAKNIFTY | EQ | 29-May-20 | 97.85 | 97.5 | 99.5 | 97 | 99.24 | 99.13 | 98.01 | | | | | |
| KOTAKNIFTY | EQ | 01-Jun-20 | 99.13 | 99.6 | 102.79 | 99.6 | 101.73 | 101.61 | 101.83 | 9979.34 | 98 | | 99862.21 | 894 | 90839.34 |
| KOTAKNIFTY | EQ | 02-Jun-20 | 101.61 | 102 | 103.4 | 101.52 | 103.28 | 103.18 | 102.63 | | | | | |
| KOTAKNIFTY | EQ | 03-Jun-20 | 103.18 | 103.5 | 107 | 103.5 | 104.01 | 104.03 | 104.88 | | | | | |
| KOTAKNIFTY | EQ | 04-Jun-20 | 104.03 | 104.35 | 105 | 102.9 | 103.68 | 103.8 | 103.59 | | | | | |
| KOTAKNIFTY | EQ | 05-Jun-20 | 103.8 | 104.09 | 105.65 | 104.03 | 105.45 | 105.02 | 104.73 | | | | | |
| KOTAKNIFTY | EQ | 08-Jun-20 | 105.02 | 106.62 | 106.8 | 105 | 105.98 | 105.29 | 106.1 | | | | | |
| KOTAKNIFTY | EQ | 09-Jun-20 | 105.29 | 105.3 | 106.9 | 99 | 104 | 104.1 | 105.37 | | | | | |
| KOTAKNIFTY | EQ | 10-Jun-20 | 104.1 | 104.45 | 105.61 | 104.33 | 105.6 | 104.94 | 104.93 | | | | | |
| KOTAKNIFTY | EQ | 11-Jun-20 | 104.94 | 104.94 | 113.9 | 102.97 | 103.5 | 103.28 | 106.74 | | | | | |
| KOTAKNIFTY | EQ | 12-Jun-20 | 103.28 | 101.98 | 103.94 | 100 | 103.75 | 103.56 | 101.72 | | | | | |
| KOTAKNIFTY | EQ | 15-Jun-20 | 103.56 | 103.22 | 103.25 | 101.02 | 102.24 | 102.13 | 102.04 | | | | | |
| KOTAKNIFTY | EQ | 16-Jun-20 | 102.13 | 106.2 | 108.92 | 101 | 102.65 | 102.74 | 103.1 | | | | | |
| KOTAKNIFTY | EQ | 17-Jun-20 | 102.74 | 103 | 103.72 | 102.2 | 102.3 | 102.56 | 102.94 | | | | | |
| KOTAKNIFTY | EQ | 18-Jun-20 | 102.56 | 102.89 | 104.9 | 102.05 | 104.16 | 104.37 | 103.7 | | | | | |
| KOTAKNIFTY | EQ | 19-Jun-20 | 104.37 | 104.9 | 106.42 | 104.49 | 106.4 | 105.88 | 105.33 | | | | | |
| KOTAKNIFTY | EQ | 22-Jun-20 | 105.88 | 105.88 | 107.39 | 105.88 | 106.7 | 106.59 | 106.75 | | | | | |
| KOTAKNIFTY | EQ | 23-Jun-20 | 106.59 | 106.54 | 108.5 | 106.54 | 108.5 | 108.2 | 107.39 | | | | | |
| KOTAKNIFTY | EQ | 24-Jun-20 | 108.2 | 108.2 | 109.21 | 106.11 | 106.95 | 106.3 | 108.02 | | | | | |
| KOTAKNIFTY | EQ | 25-Jun-20 | 106.3 | 105.99 | 107.27 | 105.6 | 105.99 | 106.05 | 106.37 | | | | | |
| KOTAKNIFTY | EQ | 26-Jun-20 | 106.05 | 106.45 | 108.07 | 106.41 | 107.99 | 107.42 | 107.16 | | | | | |

| | | | | | | | | | | | | | | |
|---|---|---|---|---|---|---|---|---|---|---|---|---|---|---|
| KOTAKNIFTY | EQ | 29-Jun-20 | 107.42 | 107.04 | 107.4 | 105.79 | 107 | 106.67 | 106.36 | | | | | |
| KOTAKNIFTY | EQ | 30-Jun-20 | 106.67 | 107 | 107.86 | 106.35 | 107 | 106.92 | 107.13 | | | | | |
| KOTAKNIFTY | EQ | 01-Jul-20 | 106.92 | 106.67 | 108.5 | 106 | 108.1 | 108.4 | 107.45 | 9992.85 | 93 | 109855.06 | 987 | 106990.8 |
| KOTAKNIFTY | EQ | 02-Jul-20 | 108.4 | 109 | 109.6 | 107.93 | 109.45 | 109.3 | 109.02 | | | | | |
| KOTAKNIFTY | EQ | 03-Jul-20 | 109.3 | 109.39 | 110.19 | 109.39 | 109.68 | 109.9 | 109.91 | | | | | |
| KOTAKNIFTY | EQ | 06-Jul-20 | 109.9 | 110.33 | 111.78 | 110.33 | 111.1 | 111.15 | 111.32 | | | | | |
| KOTAKNIFTY | EQ | 07-Jul-20 | 111.15 | 112.25 | 112.32 | 110.95 | 112.28 | 111.99 | 111.19 | | | | | |
| KOTAKNIFTY | EQ | 08-Jul-20 | 111.99 | 111.99 | 112.8 | 110.9 | 111.4 | 111.2 | 112.01 | | | | | |
| KOTAKNIFTY | EQ | 09-Jul-20 | 111.2 | 111.29 | 112.5 | 111.29 | 112.07 | 112.06 | 111.56 | | | | | |
| KOTAKNIFTY | EQ | 10-Jul-20 | 112.06 | 111.6 | 112 | 111.08 | 111.56 | 111.57 | 111.58 | | | | | |
| KOTAKNIFTY | EQ | 13-Jul-20 | 111.57 | 112.2 | 112.86 | 111.5 | 112.48 | 112.55 | 112.46 | | | | | |
| KOTAKNIFTY | EQ | 14-Jul-20 | 112.55 | 112.43 | 112.43 | 109.86 | 110.3 | 110.18 | 110.48 | | | | | |
| KOTAKNIFTY | EQ | 15-Jul-20 | 110.18 | 110.89 | 112.17 | 109.9 | 110.5 | 110.43 | 111.56 | | | | | |
| KOTAKNIFTY | EQ | 16-Jul-20 | 110.43 | 113.7 | 115.98 | 109.9 | 111.2 | 111.29 | 110.75 | | | | | |
| KOTAKNIFTY | EQ | 17-Jul-20 | 111.29 | 112 | 113.1 | 111.69 | 112.99 | 112.63 | 112.43 | | | | | |
| KOTAKNIFTY | EQ | 20-Jul-20 | 112.63 | 113 | 114.4 | 113 | 114.38 | 114.29 | 113.71 | | | | | |
| KOTAKNIFTY | EQ | 21-Jul-20 | 114.29 | 114.2 | 116.25 | 114.2 | 115.65 | 116.03 | 115.34 | | | | | |
| KOTAKNIFTY | EQ | 22-Jul-20 | 116.03 | 115.95 | 116.24 | 114.61 | 115.55 | 115.29 | 115.68 | | | | | |
| KOTAKNIFTY | EQ | 23-Jul-20 | 115.29 | 115.95 | 116.46 | 115.66 | 116.34 | 116.16 | 116.17 | | | | | |
| KOTAKNIFTY | EQ | 24-Jul-20 | 116.16 | 116.16 | 119.4 | 111.35 | 116.45 | 115.96 | 115.72 | | | | | |
| KOTAKNIFTY | EQ | 27-Jul-20 | 115.96 | 133.4 | 133.4 | 114.9 | 115.22 | 115.31 | 115.38 | | | | | |
| KOTAKNIFTY | EQ | 28-Jul-20 | 115.31 | 115 | 117.51 | 111 | 117 | 117.27 | 116.76 | | | | | |
| KOTAKNIFTY | EQ | 29-Jul-20 | 117.27 | 117.2 | 117.68 | 115.99 | 116.27 | 116.22 | 116.85 | | | | | |
| KOTAKNIFTY | EQ | 30-Jul-20 | 116.22 | 117 | 117.2 | 115.05 | 115.07 | 115.35 | 116.67 | | | | | |
| KOTAKNIFTY | EQ | 31-Jul-20 | 115.35 | 115.7 | 115.88 | 115 | 115.5 | 115.35 | 115.43 | | | | | |
| KOTAKNIFTY | EQ | 03-Aug-20 | 115.35 | 115.87 | 115.87 | 113.22 | 113.35 | 113.41 | 113.87 | 10020.56 | 88 | 119875.62 | 1075 | |
| 121915.75 | | | | | | | | | | | | | | |
| KOTAKNIFTY | EQ | 04-Aug-20 | 113.41 | 114 | 115.65 | 113.5 | 115.06 | 115.38 | 114.87 | | | | | |
| KOTAKNIFTY | EQ | 05-Aug-20 | 115.38 | 115.9 | 116.5 | 115.15 | 116 | 115.72 | 115.94 | | | | | |
| KOTAKNIFTY | EQ | 06-Aug-20 | 115.72 | 116 | 116.8 | 115.41 | 116.3 | 116.06 | 116.02 | | | | | |
| KOTAKNIFTY | EQ | 07-Aug-20 | 116.06 | 116.01 | 116.73 | 115.82 | 116.5 | 116.55 | 116.27 | | | | | |
| KOTAKNIFTY | EQ | 10-Aug-20 | 116.55 | 116.61 | 117.5 | 116.61 | 117.25 | 116.97 | 117.13 | | | | | |
| KOTAKNIFTY | EQ | 11-Aug-20 | 116.97 | 119 | 119 | 117.29 | 118 | 117.98 | 117.81 | | | | | |
| KOTAKNIFTY | EQ | 12-Aug-20 | 117.98 | 118 | 118 | 116.32 | 117.68 | 117.48 | 117.15 | | | | | |

| | | | | | | | | | | | |
|---|---|---|---|---|---|---|---|---|---|---|---|
| KOTAKNIFTY | EQ | 13-Aug-20 | 117.48 | 117.86 | 118.02 | 117.26 | 117.4 | 117.4 | 117.59 | | |
| KOTAKNIFTY | EQ | 14-Aug-20 | 117.4 | 117.56 | 118.25 | 115.8 | 116.7 | 116.31 | 117.44 | | |
| KOTAKNIFTY | EQ | 17-Aug-20 | 116.31 | 116.31 | 117.5 | 116 | 117 | 116.76 | 116.58 | | |
| KOTAKNIFTY | EQ | 18-Aug-20 | 116.76 | 117 | 118.44 | 117 | 118.4 | 118.13 | 117.83 | | |
| KOTAKNIFTY | EQ | 19-Aug-20 | 118.13 | 118.5 | 119.3 | 118.5 | 118.8 | 118.9 | 118.95 | | |
| KOTAKNIFTY | EQ | 20-Aug-20 | 118.9 | 118.9 | 118.9 | 117.21 | 117.8 | 117.81 | 117.79 | | |
| KOTAKNIFTY | EQ | 21-Aug-20 | 117.81 | 118.8 | 119 | 117.97 | 118.1 | 118.1 | 118.38 | | |
| KOTAKNIFTY | EQ | 24-Aug-20 | 118.1 | 119.08 | 119.25 | 118.41 | 119 | 118.99 | 118.86 | | |
| KOTAKNIFTY | EQ | 25-Aug-20 | 118.99 | 119.25 | 119.58 | 118.79 | 119.22 | 119.12 | 119.32 | 28 Aug 20 value at close | 129935.25 |
| KOTAKNIFTY | EQ | 26-Aug-20 | 119.12 | 119.55 | 120 | 119.02 | 119.99 | 119.98 | 119.39 | Basic Value | 119875.62 |
| KOTAKNIFTY | EQ | 27-Aug-20 | 119.98 | 120.04 | 120.6 | 120.01 | 120.1 | 120.1 | 120.31 | Profit / Loss | 10059.63 |
| KOTAKNIFTY | EQ | 28-Aug-20 | 120.1 | 120.33 | 121.14 | 120.33 | 121 | 120.87 | 120.83 | Profit in percentage | 8.391723021 |
| | | | | | | | | | | | 16% |

# APPENDIX-G

**Monthaly 2 Percent Return Calculator**

| | installment | total investment | 2% | |
|---|---|---|---|---|
| Sep-19 | 10000 | 10000 | 200 | |
| Oct-19 | 10000 | 20000 | 400 | |
| Nov-19 | 10000 | 30000 | 600 | |
| Dec-19 | 10000 | 40000 | 800 | |
| Jan-20 | 10000 | 50000 | 1000 | |
| Feb-20 | 10000 | 60000 | 1200 | |
| Mar-20 | 10000 | 70000 | 1400 | |
| Apr-20 | 10000 | 80000 | 1600 | |
| May-20 | 10000 | 90000 | 1800 | |
| Jun-20 | 10000 | 100000 | 2000 | |
| Jul-20 | 10000 | 110000 | 2200 | |
| Aug-20 | 10000 | 120000 | 2400 | |
| | | | **15600** | 24% |

❑

# 6

# Sovereign Gold Bond vs Gold ETF

Gold ETFs are ETFs based on gold price. Gold ETF prices do not fluctuate much. But even today Gold ETFs trade more on NSE than other ETFs on the basis of volume.

Gold anyway has always had a special traditional significance for Indians. They do not see the percentage of return from investment in Gold ETFs in India because there is a need to buy gold at the time of marriages and other special life events. It is almost essential for traditional jewellery in India. That's why people feel that even if the prices of Gold ETFs fall, they will buy physical gold with the amount received by selling the ETF.

Therefore, buying gold should not be treated as buying based on ordinary shares.

A common Indian believes that gold should be bought when it is cheap. Hence Gold ETF unit should also be bought when it is available at a discount. But since the movement in the price of gold is very slow, like equities, it is difficult to determine the discount.

So, in this chapter you will learn such a method of SIP in Gold by which you will benefit both ways.

In India, if we talk about the majority, a person needs gold at the time of the wedding of his or her children. Let's say, your son or daughter is 12 years old now and you consider their estimated age of marriage to be 24 years. That'll be when you might need the amount to buy gold.

So, you should invest in Sovereign Gold Bonds instead of investing in gold ETFs. The Reserve Bank of India issues Sovereign Gold Bonds every month on behalf of the Government of India.

These gold bonds are issued at a face value equal to 1 gram of gold. In these, the price is equal to 1 gram of gold. But their biggest feature is that the Government of India also gives you 2.5% interest annually.

I used a phrase at the beginning of this chapter- 'You will benefit both ways'. It meant that if the value of gold increases after investing in Sovereign Gold Bonds, then the value of these bonds also increases. But even if the value does not increase, the interest is paid on it by the Government of India at the rate of 2.5% annually.

The interest gets credited to the bank account linked to your Demat account on a half-yearly basis.

You can directly buy Sovereign Gold Bond through RBI. When the issue is open, the issue of Sovereign Gold Bond also appears on your broker's website in the same way like an IPO.

There are 6 major advantages of investing in Sovereign Gold Bonds:

1. Since it is issued by the Government of India, the investment is safer than other private bonds as the investment in it is guaranteed by the government.

2. With the increase in the price of gold, the price of the bond also increases. The duration of the bond is 8 years. After 8 years, you get paid at the current price of gold. One bond is equal to 1 gram of gold. You can also receive payment according to the market price of gold before 8 years as these bonds trade like shares on the NSE website. So, you can exit at any time by selling them like shares at the current market price (which is almost equal to the current price of gold).

3. Your investment also gives a return of 2.5% per annum, which is not less considering the present

time (this book was written in 2021). At present, 3% return is available in a savings account and a 5-6% in a bank FD. Compared to that, this return is not less because you get the benefit of increase in the value of gold along with a 2.5% interest.

4. Capital gains in this maturity are exempt from income tax as per the existing rules. At present, if you hold a Sovereign Gold Bond till maturity and take the returns according to the increase in the value of gold after 8 years, then your income is tax free. If you buy Sovereign Gold Bonds through trading in the secondary market and not directly in issue, your income is subject to long term capital gains tax after getting indexation benefit, which is negligible as indexation benefit is available.

5. If you buy gold and keep it in the house, then there is a fear of it being stolen. But you can hold a Sovereign Gold Bond in a Demat account.

6. Margin can be obtained on this bond by pledging it with your broker as collateral. With this margin you can trade in shares. If you hold Sovereign Gold Bonds equal to the minimum lot size of gold in options trading, you can safely earn monthly income by writing covered calls of Gold Options.

If you want to know more about options trading, writing a covered call, you can read my book *How to Plant a Money Tree with Options Trading*.

Apart from this, loans can also be obtained from banks by pledging them with banks at about 80% of their value.

Sovereign Gold Bonds are also traded on NSE like stocks.

Let me explain with an example of a Sovereign Gold Bond maturing in March 2024 to make things clearer:

This bond was issued in 2016, 8 years before the maturity date, at ₹ 2916 as per the market price of 1 gram of gold.

In May 2021, it was trading on the NSE website for ₹ 4,800. Its NSE code is SGBMAR24, where SGB stands for Sovereign Gold Bond and MAR24 is its maturity month.

You would have taken it in March 2016 for ₹ 2916 and if you needed the money in May 2021, you could have sold it for ₹ 4,800. In 2016, the government used to issue it at 2.75% interest per annum instead of 2.5%. So, for the past 5 years, you would have got 2.75% annual interest (half-yearly) also in your account. The overall point is that compared to Gold ETFs, it is better to invest an SIP in Sovereign Gold Bonds.

Now I will explain how to start this SIP. Suppose your daughter or son is 12 years old, you will need to gold during the time of his or her marriage.

You consider the estimated marital age to be 24 years. It is 2021 now and your son or daughter will be 24 years old in 2033.

So, you kept buying Sovereign Gold Bonds of 1-1 grams per month from 2021 to 2025 with a maturity of 8 years.

Now the March 2025 bond will mature in March 2033. After that, from April 2025 to February 2033, you keep buying 1-1 bonds with maturity of March 2033 from the secondary market every month so that all the bonds bought after March 2025 together will mature in March 2033. As you keep getting the maturity amount from the bonds purchased from April 2021 to February 2025, keep investing them in the bonds with maturity of March 2033 from NSE. Thus, by March 2033, you will have 144 grams of gold bonds purchased in 12 years (1 gram per month to 12 grams in 12 months and 144 grams in 12 years), whose maturity amount will be given to you at the market price of gold. With this you will be able to buy 144 grams of gold for the wedding.

Apart from this, you will also continue to get regular income on these bonds at the rate of 2.5% per annum interest during these 12 years.

## Summary

1. Sovereign Gold Bond is the safest investment option in gold.
2. It offers the benefit of increasing the value of gold along with a coupon rate of 2.5% per annum.
3. With this, 1-1 grams of gold can be collected from the SIP method at the time of the wedding.

❑

# 7

# Importance of SIP in the Debt Market

Many of my readers may also have heard the names of REITs and INVITs, Treasury Bills, Sovereign Bonds and Corporate Bonds for the first time. Some readers may have only superficial knowledge about them and some readers will be reluctant to invest in them even though they have more knowledge because they may believe that there is no special benefit in them.

I advise all the above readers to read this chapter very carefully as you will find many such pieces of information in it which will change your earlier view about investing in the debt market.

If you have seen the web series based on Harshad Mehta, then you must have also heard the dialogue –

'Debt market has 3 times more turnover than equity market'. (During Harshad Mehta's time, the debt market used to have 3 times more turnover than the equity market. Nowadays, it has 5 times more turnover). There must be something about this market as 5 times more capital is invested in it than in the stock market.

In fact, the reason why the debt market is not very popular among the common people is that it is difficult for small investors like me with low net worth to enter because the minimum lot amount of Corporate Bonds, Sovereign Bonds, Bonds of Government of India, Bonds of State Governments and Treasury Bills etc, ranges from 1 lakh to 10 lakhs. In such a situation, for investing in 1-1 bonds, you have to invest 1 to 10 lakh rupees. Due to this large lot size, the common investor is not able to invest in the debt market. Hence this market remains a major attraction for the high-net-worth investors.

Now you will ask what is special about this? It gives almost the same return as a bank FD. If you think so, then it is wrong. In this chapter, I will tell you the advantages of investing in the debt market and in the next two chapters, I will tell you how you can invest in the debt market with less capital through an SIP.

Let us look at the major advantages of investing in the debt market

1. Due to the fixed returns of bonds, etc like a bank FD, the investment made in it does not fluctuate like equity and there is less possibility of losing the original capital in comparison to the equity market.

2. In the debt market, sovereign bonds are issued by the Government of India and various state governments; they are less risky due to the sovereign guarantee of the state governments on investment.

3. At present the bank interest rates have come down to a very low level. Now only 3.5% interest is being available in the savings account of banks, which is negligible considering the inflation rate.

Now let's talk about REITs (Real Estate Investment Trust) and INVITs (Infrastructure Investment Trust) first. You must be thinking that REITs and INVITs are very advanced investment methods, which might have come into vogue only in the last few years. But it is not so at all. You will be surprised and sad to know that in the US, the trend of REITs and INVITs started around 1960, whereas in our country the public is not aware about it even in 2021. So, from this point of view, we lag behind by sixty years.

Both are types of mutual funds, in which the investor collects his money and gives it to a trust, which invests that money in real estate projects (in case of REITs in real estate projects) or infrastructure projects (in case of

INVITs in infrastructure projects). After the creation of the said property, 90% of the rent earned by the trust is required to be distributed to these trusts in the form of dividends among the investors.

Also, these trusts cannot invest more than 20% of their capital in under-construction projects, in debt funds, in bonds of real estate companies. By doing this, it is ensured that these companies invest 80% of their capital in projects that have been completed, thereby ensuring regular income to their investors.

For example, in the year 2020, Embassy Office Parks REIT distributed the income as follows:

1. Rs 6.10 per unit as on 20th January, 2020
2. Rs 6.89 per unit as on 27th May, 2020
3. Rs 5.83 per unit as on 13th August, 2020
4. Rs 5.50 per unit as on 9th November, 2020

From this you can guess that a unit of about ₹ 300 has earned an income of ₹ 4.32 in a year. Therefore, along with the regular income, one can also get capital gains on increasing unit price.

Units of REITs and INVITs are traded in the stock exchanges like shares. At present there are 3 REITs and 2 INVITs listed in Indian stock exchanges NSE and BSE. Their names and their market prices as on 23rd April, 2021 are as follows:

**REITs:**

1. Embassy Office Parks REIT–Market Price 310.48 as of 23rd April, 2021
2. Mindspace Business Parks REIT–Market Price 298 as on 23rd April, 2021
3. Brookfield India REIT –Market Price 241.62, as on 23rd April 2021

**INVITs:**

1. India Grid Trust –Market Value 130 as on 23rd April, 2021
2. IRB Invit Fund –Market Price 52.88 as on 23rd April, 2021

Now the problem is that SEBI has fixed the minimum lot size in the shares of Real Estate and Infrastructure Investment Trusts, that is, you cannot include them in your portfolio by buying 1, 2, 10, 50 or 100 shares in them like the shares of other companies.

At present the minimum lot size in REITs is at least 200 shares, ie, if you want to invest in any of the three REIT'S mentioned above and if its current market value is ₹ 300 then you will have to invest minimum 200×300 = ₹ 60,000 at a time.

Similarly, the lot size of India Grid Trust Invit is 1701 shares, that is, to invest in it at the market price of 125, you have to invest approximately 2,12,625 together.

At present, the minimum lot size in REITs is at least 200 shares, ie, you have to invest in any of the three REIT'S mentioned above and if its current market value is ₹ 300 then you have to invest minimum 200 × 300 = ₹ 60,000. If you do not want to invest 60,000 in one go, the only way for you is to do a monthly SIP in a mutual fund that has holdings in all these REITs and INVITs.

REITs and INVITs are still in their very early stages in Indian stock markets. Right now, some government companies like NTPC, POWR GRID etc, are also going to bring their own INVITs. By the time this book is in your hands, some new REITs and INVITs will also have entered the market.

Currently, in the Indian markets, mutual funds in the Hybrid Mutual Fund or Aggressive Hybrid Mutual Fund category are mutual funds that invest in REITs and INVITs. A hybrid mutual fund is a mutual fund that invests in both equity and debt. Therefore, for those who do not have a huge amount like ₹ 60,000 to 1 lakh to invest in REITs and INVITs together or who do not want to invest such a huge amount together, for them investing in Hybrid (especially Aggressive Hybrid) Mutual Funds through SIP can be the better option.

Although I, the author of this book, am a SEBI Registered Research Analyst, I am not a mutual fund advisor. Therefore, this chapter written to enhance your knowledge should not be taken as an advice to invest in mutual funds.

Now many readers will ask the question – what will be the return on investing in an Aggressive Hybrid Mutual Fund? Though investing in Mutual Funds is always subject to market risks, the 5-year CAGR of SBI Equity Hybrid Fund return was 13.24% as of April 2021 at the time of writing this book.

In the coming times, such mutual funds or ETFs can also be launched in the Indian stock markets which are completely based on investment in REITs and INVITs. Apart from this, there is another option that if you are already investing in equity at your level or you are already investing in equity mutual funds, then you can choose pure debt funds instead of hybrid mutual funds.

Now we will discuss Debt Mutual Funds, which invest in Bonds, Treasury Bills as well as Corporate Bonds and REITs and INVITs. Corporate Bonds Funds are similar debt mutual funds that invest in Treasury Bills, Sovereign Gold Bonds and also in REIT'S and INVIT'S.

I personally invest ₹ 5,000 per month as a SIP in SBI Corporate Bonds Fund continuously because:

1. I prefer to invest in government mutual funds like SBI and it is because of people like me that you will see that SBI Mutual Fund schemes in India have the

largest number of investments and assets managed by them.

2. This corporate bond fund gives an annual return of around 8 to 10%.

3. With just a monthly investment of ₹ 5,000, I get an opportunity to invest in Treasury Bills, Sovereign Gold Bonds and also in REITs and INVITs.

4. Sometimes the stock market falls and I need money. Then at that time, I will not need to sell the shares at a loss. I can get money by selling the units of this Corporate Bond Fund.

5. Being an open-ended fund, there is no lock in period.

6. If I put my surplus money in FD in SBI, I would get 5 to 6% interest. Even on this interest, I would have to pay income tax so that my actual return would have been only 3 to 4% because of my 30% income tax slab, while my amount invested in SBI Corporate Fund would have no income till I sold the unit. I do not havc to pay incomc tax and the day I need money, I will sell the unit. Then I will get the benefit of indexation on it, that is, on the basis of increased inflation, if I get anything by reducing the inflation rate, only then will I have to pay income tax.

Therefore, after paying income tax on their earnings, the middle-class investors put the rest of the amount in a bank FD and again pay income tax on the interest of that FD. Due to this, they start falling short of money due to the increasing inflation, due to which they take other people's FD money from banks as loan and pay more interest. In this way, they keep dreaming of getting rich by paying interest and income tax. But the upper-class people invest their money in Corporate Bonds Fund and take indexation benefit of the rising inflation on its returns so that their savings are able to compete well with inflation.

So, don't forget what you read in your childhood that greed is bad. No matter how much profit you see in equity funds, balance your investments and keep at least the same number of SIPs in debt funds as you are doing in equity funds. My choice among debt funds is corporate bond funds. Further, mutual funds and ETFs based solely on investment in REITs and INVITs may also enter the market. Then I'd prefer to invest in them as well.

❑

# 8

# SIP in ETFs instead of Mutual Funds

First, we have to understand what an ETF is. The literal meaning of ETFs is Exchange Traded Funds, that is, they are mutual funds that can be bought and sold on a stock exchange like stocks. But there is a fundamental difference between ETFs and mutual funds. The fund manager has to keep in mind that their portfolio remains exactly the same as the index.

As Nifty Seeds is a Nifty based ETF. In this, the fund manager will buy all the 50 shares of Nifty in the same ratio as they are earmarked for Nifty. Due to this, if Nifty rises, then naturally the NAV (Net Asset Value).of Nifty seed will also increase. Remember here that the market price of an ETF that is traded like a stock means its NAV.

Ideally, the price of one unit of Nifty seed is kept equal to 1/100 of Nifty. As on 7th April, 2020 the value of Nifty was 8,493.90. Then ideally the market value of Nifty seed would have been ₹ 84.94. But that day it was trading around ₹ 90. Small investors simply do not understand this fact. They often ask me by commenting/e-mailing why the price of Nifty seed does not move exactly 1/100 of Nifty? Basically, ETF is neither a mutual fund nor a stock. It is a combination of mutual fund and stock. That is, if Nifty Seed ETF was a mutual fund, then its ideal NAV would be 1/100 of Nifty. But due to its being an ETF, when it trades like shares, then its price is also determined as per demand-supply system. That is, when the market is expected to increase and there are more buyers, then it starts trading at a premium. This is the reason why it is trading at 90 instead of 84 because due to bullish trend, the premium starts running and due to low demand in the market in the bearish trend, it is possible that Nifty is at 8,300 and Nifty seed is trading at 80 only. Overall, 1/100 of Nifty is its fair value. But the actual price depends on the demand and supply. Now let's come back to the fundamental difference between ETFs and Mutual Funds. The proportion of shares in an ETF is kept roughly the same as the underlying index. But it is not necessary to do this in mutual funds. In this, the mutual fund manager can completely leave any stock in the index on which the fund is based, eg, if a mutual fund is a large cap fund and a mutual fund related to Nifty 50, then it is the will of the fund manager that they take only a few shares out of the Nifty 50 shares, or take all the shares or take more of some shares and take less of some. But the number and ratio of shares in an ETF is kept the same as the underlying index.

Now let's talk about whether one can invest in an SIP in ETFs? The answer is that some brokers and online trading platforms offer systematic equity plans wherein you can invest a fixed monthly amount in large blue-chip stocks/ select stocks like mutual funds. So, if your broker or your trading platform allows SIP in ETFs from Systematic Equity Plans, you can. Otherwise, you will have to do an SIP manually by buying ETF for a specified amount every month on a specified date for an SIP in ETF.

## Summary

1. An ETF is a type of basket of shares that is traded on an exchange like an independent stock.
2. It is safer to buy mutual fund units or buy ETFs than stocks alone.
3. You can also do an SIP in ETFs like mutual funds. But if your broker does not provide this facility then you may have to undertake this SIP manually like buying shares.

❑

# 9

# Choosing an ETF for Investment or SIP?

Many investors want to invest in ETFs through SIP. By investing in ETFs, they can easily keep up with the index. Currently ETFs based not only on Nifty 50 are available in the market, but now on NSE in the stock market of India, there are ETFs available based on the Bank Nifty, CPSE Index, Nifty Next 50, Junior Nifty, Bharat 22, Gold, Nifty IT, Sensex, Mid Cap and Nasdaq. Nasdaq is the index of America. So, the fun part is that you can enjoy investing in top US companies sitting at home with Nasdaq ETFs. As the concept of ETFs for the stock markets of India was new, ETFs did not have volume in the initial few years, due to which traders and small investors were hesitant to buy ETFs seeing low volumes.

But since the shares of big companies like Yes Bank, India Bulls broke badly in the stock market, common investors also felt that it is safer to invest in the basket of shares ETF than investing in any one company. Also, investors who wanted to invest in all the stocks of Nifty/ Bank Nifty together, their trend increased in ETFs as well. So now-a-days, increasing volumes are being seen in ETFs. The basis for selecting an ETF can be its underlying index and its volume.

From time to time, I share a diversified portfolio of top 10-12 ETFs with the highest volume on my YouTube channel. Currently (June 2021 when this book was written), these 10 ETFs in India have been selected by me on the basis of their volume and diversification (Keep visiting my YouTube channel for updates from time to time):

| S. No. | Underlying Index |
|---|---|
| 1. | NSE Code of ETF: NIFTYBEES, Underlying Index: Nifty |
| 2. | NSE Code of ETF: BANKBEES, Underlying Index: Nifty Bank |
| 3. | NSE Code of ETF: CPSEETF, Underlying Index: CPSE Index |
| 4. | NSE Code of ETF: ICICIB22, Underlying Index: Bharat 22 |
| 5. | NSE Code of ETF: NETFIT, Underlying Index: Nifty IT |
| 6. | NSE Code of ETF: NETFMID150, Underlying Index: Nifty Midcap 150 |
| 7. | NSE Code of ETF: JUNEERBEES, Underlying Index: Nifty Next 50 |
| 8. | NSE Code of ETF: SBIETFQUALITY, Underlying Index: Nifty 200 Quality 30 |
| 9. | NSE Code of ETF: N100 ETF, Underlying Index: NASDAQ |

| | |
|---|---|
| 10. | NSE Code of ETF: M100, Underlying Index: Nifty Midcap 100 |
| 11. | NSE Code of ETF: ICICIs00 ETF, Underlying Index: BSE 500 |
| 12. | NSE Code of ETF: GOLDBEES, Underhying Index: Gold |

As you can see that the above 12 ETFs have high volumes and their underlying indexes are so diversified that SIPs done in these 12 ETFs can help you invest in most of the top companies in India and America and gold as well. Keep in mind, the above list is for the sake familiarity only. You have not been advised here to invest in the said ETFs. Before investing, you should check your risk-taking ability and choose the fund on the basis of your own research because investing in the stock market is always subject to market risks.

## Summary

1. If the ETF is selected on the basis of its volume, then there is a facility to buy/sell the units.
2. The N100 is an ETF based on the NASDAQ US Index.
3. In addition to doing an SIP in ETFs like mutual funds, they can also be traded like shares.
4. ETFs like GOLDBEES are based on the price of gold.

❑

# 10

# SRNTV Strategy for Investing in and Exiting Mutual Funds

This chapter is very special. With the knowledge that I am going to share with you, I am sure I'll receive a 5-star review of my book. This is the result of my in depth research on SIP in Mutual Funds and ETFs, due to which I was able to discover the SRNTV method.

It is seen that the market falls twice in a year on an average, ie, once or twice a year there is such a phase of decline in the market when you can buy shares/Mutual Funds, ETFs at very cheap prices. But the common investor is not able to catch this fall. He thinks in a downtrend that the market is going to fall further and during a bullish period, he thinks that the market is going to rise further.

The common investor has no tool to measure whether the market is bullish or bearish. He can neither buy shares in recession nor book profit in bullish momentum. I did a lot of research to solve this dilemma. Then I came to the conclusion that if you can time the market, then your lump sum investment in downtrend can give you much higher returns than a monthly SIP.

This led to the discovery of SRNTV, which in its full form can be called Share Genius Ratio of Nifty Technical Valuation. To calculate this, we assume that the market will be either very low or very high twice in a year. Now suppose there are 365 days in a year, out of which on subtracting 52 Saturdays and 52 Sundays, 261 days are left. On an average, 13 days in a year are market holidays like Diwali, Eid-ul-Zuha, Mahavir Jayanti and others. Now if we subtract 13 out of these 261 days, then the stock market opens for about 248 days in a year.

Now we will further divide these 248 days by 2 because we believe that 2 times in a year there are big downslides in the market. So, dividing 248 by 2 gives us the number 124. Now we will download the Historical Price Data of Nifty from the NSE website. If you do not know how to download the Historical Price Data of Nifty, then you can learn it from my YouTube channel. Now to calculate the Nifty Share Genius Ratio of Nifty Technical Valuation, you can use the following formula:

SRNTV = Close Price of Nifty/124 DMA (Direct Market Access) of Nifty

(DMA is very easy to calculate. Just like you calculate average in maths, you can easily calculate DMA by entering the excel formula in the price data that you have downloaded in the excel sheet.)

In Appendix 'F' of this book, I am providing you the data of the close price of Nifty and its 124 DMA and close price/124 DMA from 1st April, 2005 to 12th May, 2017.

You can see the data for its calculation sheet, 124 DMA and close price/124 DMA in Appendix-D given at the end of the book.

Going through this Appendix-E, you can go through the data of SRNTV ie, Close Price/124 DMA. You will learn:

1. The value of SRNTV has never been less than 0.59 in the last 12 years.
2. The value of SRNTV never exceeded 1.46 in the last 12 years.
3. The value between this maximum value of 1.46 and the minimum value of 0.59 is 1.03

ie:

1. If the SRNTV ratio is around 1.03, i.e. 1.00, 1.01, 1.02, 1.03, 1.04, 1.05, 1.06, then the market

valuation is neither too expensive nor too cheap. At this valuation, you should neither book profit on the units of the old investment nor initiate a new investment. This time can neither be called bullish time nor can it be called bearish time. Its time to wait and watch.

2. We can divide SRNTV's midpoint 1.03 and minimum point 0.59 into 5 different levels. These levels will each be 0.09 points below 1.03:

   i. **Level of 0.94:** This is the first level of decline. Here if you want to invest 1 lakh in the market, then invest 1/5 of it in 0.20 lakh or twenty thousand mutual funds or ETFs. Many times, the market bounces back due to recession and if this happens then you will get a good return on this investment in a very short time. It is usually seen once a year.

   ii. **0.85 Level:** This is the level of deepening of the downslide in the market. This level is likely to come every 2 to 3 years. So, at this stage also keep 1/5 amount ready for investment.

   iii. **0.76 Level:** It falls in major downtrends, such as the fall of 2008 and 2020. The amount should be kept ready for investment here and 1/5 amount should be invested.

iv. **0.67 Level:** This level is a sign of the market becoming heavily undervalued. During this also, 1/5 amount should be invested.

v. **0.59 Level:** This is the rarest level. In 2008 also, the minimum level was 0.59. Therefore, if the market seems to have fallen so much that there is an SRNTV of 0.59, then 1/5 of the amount should be invested. Similarly on the contrary, i.e. at 1.12, 1.21, 1.30, 1.39, 1.48 at 1.12, 1.21, 1.30, 1.48, one fifth of your original mutual fund holdings at 1.12, 1.21, 1.30, 1.39, at levels above 1.03 each must sell at 1.48 level.

Now you will say, 'Sir, this seems so complicated. Who will fuss over the multiplication?'

The answer is that I keep updating as and when such levels arise through my YouTube channel and blog. In my automated sheet with 100 DMA, the link of which is given on my blog, I have also put an auto-updated formula for this ratio so that you can check this ratio daily in that sheet. Some even simpler methods will be described for you in subsequent chapters.

## Summary

1. SRNTV is a parameter by which Nifty (Over All Market) is undervalued or overvalued.

2. Wait for SRNTV to drop below 0.94 before starting a new SIP. If you do not want to get involved in the multiplication, then all you need to do is start an SIP if SRNTV is below 0.94.

3. If you are sitting on a lot of profit in mutual fund, then some profit must be booked after SRNTV rises above 1.12. Once its above 1.12 you can start a Systematic Withdrawal Plan.

4. SRNTV has a 1.03 average level. 0.94 level is achieved only once or twice in a year. Levels below that are found only in large falls. Similarly, the level of 1.12 is common in the uptrend, but the levels above that are found only in a much bigger bullish trend.

❑

# 11

# Booking Profits in Mutual Funds

I have been working in the share market since 2005. I have seen from my vast experience of 15 years that when the stock market is in a bullish trend, everyone starts enumerating the advantages of Long-Term SIP (Systematic Equity Plan) that if you had invested 10 years back then your fund value today would have been so high. Everyone says in a chorus that its not the time to book profit, one should stay in an equity or mutual fund, that there will be more growth etc... etc.

But just as happiness and sorrow, profit and loss, life and death are part of the eternal cycle, so are the ups and downs part of the cycle of the market. When there are declines like 1930, 1992, 2000, 2008, 2018, 2020, then the investors whose mutual fund portfolio is in profit of lakhs of rupees, start losing the entire benefit in the fall.

I have always been a proponent of booking reasonable profits at the right time. In this book, I have told you about the monthly income method by booking profit. The second method that I told you about is SRNTV. But due to the complexity of both these methods, the common investor will still ask me, "Is there any other simple method to book profit in an SIP of mutual funds apart from the above two methods?"

So, the answer is yes. There is a very simple method. Whenever the units of your mutual fund SIP which are more than one year old come into above 15% profit, then book profit in everything except the units purchased in the last 12 months and let the SIP continue. You will ask, "Why is that so?"

That's because:

1. You get 6 to 7% return in a Bank FD. That too attracts income tax, whereas long-term capital gains up to ₹ 1 lakh in mutual fund units sold after holding it for more than 1 year are exempt from income tax. So, if 1 year old unit is getting 15% tax free profit then it is better to book profit immediately without consulting an astrologer.
2. The figure of 15% has also not been taken randomly. If you look at the history of the last 30 years, the stock markets around the world have given an

average return of only about 15% annually. Then why do you expect above-average returns?

Now many readers, who have not read this book from the beginning, will ask the same question mentioned in the previous chapters, "Sir, in this way, I will be deprived of the benefits of a long-term SIP. I have heard that in a long term SIP, due to the power of compound interest, crores of rupees can be made. But you are booking profit in only 15%. Then how will my fund of crores of rupees be made?"

Answer: If you really want to invest in an SIP in the long term, then there is a method for that, too. After you book the profit in 15% itself, invest the total recovered amount along with the profit in a corporate bond fund.

Corporate Bond Fund is a type of debt fund, through which one can easily get higher returns than bank FDs.

Now you have to withdraw 1/12 of this amount every month from the Corporate Bond Fund and add it to your already issued SIP amount and invest it back with a new SIP of the total amount. It has been described in detail in the previous chapters.

## Summary

1. By booking profit from time to time in mutual funds, one can keep his profit safe from market downturns.

2. If you are getting 15% return on units held for more than 1 year, then it is better to take it.

3. The long-term annual average return of stock markets around the world is approximately 15%.

4. As per the current income tax rules, long term capital gains up to ₹ 1 lakh per annum are exempt from tax if you book profit by selling equity mutual fund units held for more than a year. After that, income tax has to be paid on it at the rate of 10%. Income tax rules keep changing. Therefore, whenever you read this book, you must get the information about the rules prevailing at that particular time from the website of the Income Tax Department.

❑

# 12

# The Babylon Method of Mutual Fund SIP

Now let me introduce you to the Babylon method of SIP. I understand the name Babylonian Law may be strange and unfamiliar to your ears. Basically, this method is based on the eternal knowledge of wealth obtained from another ancient book. The name of that ancient book is *The Richest Man of Babylon*. I have been advising my followers to read this book from time to time. So, if you are my old follower then you must have read this book. If you have heard about this book from me for the first time, then I advise you to read the aforementioned book once after reading this book. It'll give you a good knowledge of the eternal laws of wealth.

Apart from the Babylonian method, there's another method called Build your own Bank method, I'd like to share. In this, investment/profit booking has been managed in a very systematic manner. But to follow this system, it is very important for you to follow financial discipline. In this method, first we have to understand who the rich man is. What is the definition of a really rich person? Who is really rich? For this, the first thing is that the definition of a rich man cannot be determined by his net worth.

Like when we were young, being a millionaire was a big deal. Then a handful of millionaires came up in every village. Then being a billionaire became a big deal. Some would call a billionaire person rich. So, the real measure of being rich should never be done by his net worth.

Although many readers may disagree with my statement in my clear opinion, being rich cannot be defined. But by comparative study, it can be identified who is richer and who is really rich. I will explain this to you by giving examples of three imaginary people:

1. Mr. Rajuram
2. Mr. Shankarlal
3. Mr. Shailendra Singh

## Now let's get introduced to them.

1. Mr. Rajuram is a wholesale grocery trader. He supplies biscuits, snacks, toffee, tea, sugar packets to

retail traders. He uses a bicycle and lives in a simple house. He wears plain clothes and his chappals are worth ₹ 35. He uses an ordinary mobile phone. He drinks buttermilk. There is approximately ₹ 67 lakh in his bank, including cash and fixed deposits.

2. Mr. Shankarlal: He is a farmer. He received 40 bighas of agricultural land as his share, which was ancestral property. But fortunately, due to the highway passing through this land, its market price rose to approximately 50 lakh/bigha. The farmer got ₹ 5 crore by selling 10 bighas out of 40 bighas of land. From that money, he built a luxurious house and bought many amenities like a car and so on. He cultivates only the remaining 30 bighas of land. He has only ₹ 2130 in his bank. The market value of his house and remaining 30 bighas of land is around 20 crores.

3. Mr. Shailendra Singh: He works in a private company. He gets a monthly salary of 50,000. But most of the salary is spent on expensive mobiles, expensive shoes, fashionable clothes, expensive liquor. Due to the overdraft of credit card, he has a balance of (-) 200 rupees in the bank account. The real estate property is nil.

Now if I ask you who is the richest of these three, you will naturally say that the richest person is the farmer

Shankarlal. But in my humble opinion, Shankarlal farmer may be rich in net worth but he is not really rich because according to me only person with liquid capital is really rich. Liquid capital means the capital that you can use when needed.

Now Shankarlal farmer has a bungalow and car worth 5 crores. But if he sells it when needed, his family will be homeless. Also, they will not get the customer for the house and car immediately. The third problem will be that customers will try to take advantage of their situation and try to buy his property at throwaway prices. Sometimes such a property is not sold for upto 5 years due to the no offer of a reasonable price being made.

So, Shankarlal farmer may be rich in net worth, but he is not really rich because according to me, the only person with liquid capital is the really rich person. That means Rajuram whose liquid capital is 67 lakhs is really the richest person of all. In fact, the sale of immovable property/material goods etc. is uncertain. Their market price is also uncertain and it is also not certain if it will be sold at the time of need. So, first you have to understand that a person with more liquid capital is the truly rich person.

Now it is also to be understood that holding units of mutual funds in the equity market is also liquid capital because if needed, by selling them at the market price, the amount can be obtained in 2 to 3 days. So, if you hold cash/ equity units/gold, then these are all assets that determine real wealth. Now the simplest part of this method is to invest 90% of what you earn in your daily needs and save the remaining 10% for SIP.

I know that after reading this sentence, many of my readers will feel annoyed that there was so much ado about nothing. You will say that to explain such a thing, why did I make such a huge background unnecessarily? My dear readers, it is not as trivial as you think. To absorb this rather serious matter, read some of the points given below and ponder on them:

1. Some readers will say that they are hardly able to meet the daily needs. They are not able to save even 5% from their income. They are in debt etc. Those readers will doubt that it is not only difficult but impossible for them to save 10% of their monthly income.

   It was for these readers that I had initially advised the book *The Rich Man of Babylon* to be read. But even if you haven't read the book, you should remember that economists all over the world are unanimous in the view that if you can run the house with ₹ 100 then the same can be done with ₹ 90. Decreasing the budget to 90 from 100 will make very little difference in your daily needs and expenses.

2. It is also an eternal law or take it as a spiritual law that as soon as you start saving 10% of your income, there is also an unexpected increase in your income from some source or the other. This law cannot be explained by any science. It can be experienced only by doing it in practice. Strictly try to save 10% of your monthly income every month. You will experience the miracle of unexpected increase in your income in 3 months. Many of my followers have experienced this as well. Although this is not guaranteed to happen and assuming nothing of the sort happens as your income increases, saving 10% isn't going to take a lot of effort either.

3. When you think of an SIP or start an SIP, then a natural question comes to your mind– 'How much money should I invest in an SIP per month?' The second question will be– 'How much amount should I increase in an SIP every year?' The Babylonian method gives a natural answer to both your questions– 'You should invest in an SIP every month, an amount equal to 10% of your monthly income.'

   For example, if your monthly income is ₹ 57,000 per month then SIP of 5700/- per month is the most appropriate and most ideal situation for you. If you invest in an SIP less than that ie, 3000/- per month, then it will be insufficient for your future needs and lifestyle. If you have more than this ie, 10,000 per month SIP, you may have to break and stop your SIP soon to meet your needs.

Similarly, if you earn only 5,000 per month then an SIP of 500 is the most ideal and most suitable for you. Now as the income increases, this will also keep increasing, eg, as the income increases from 5,000 to 6000 per month. If the income increases to 10,000 per month, then increase the SIP to 1000 per month. If you strictly follow this 10% rule, you will soon have a corpus that will be high for you (the amount added from SIP of 5000 per month can be small for groups like Tata, Birla, Ambani, but that would be a huge sum of money for you).

Now here I remember a story, which will be very interesting and informative for you to hear. Near my house, there is a grocer called Shri Yogendraji. I often go to him to buy incense sticks and other necessities. I gifted him *The Rich Man of Babylon*. After he read it I asked him, "How was it?"

He said, "It was very nice."

I asked, "So, you're going to save 10% of your income from tomorrow, aren't you?" He said, "No sir, I can't."

I asked, "Why?"

So, at first, he made excuses like the business is not doing too well, and that he is barely able to run his house, etc. Then I assured him that if he saved 10% for just 3 months, then the sales of the shop will automatically increase. He said that he did not even know how much his monthly income was. I was very surprised. I said that he could note down the sales in the shop throughout the day and put it aside in the evening and set aside 10%.

Now Yogendraji reasoned that suppose by evening the sale was worth ₹ 2000, then that sum wasn't be his income as it would include the original cost of the goods.

I found this argument of Yogendra to be justified. I said, "It doesn't matter, but you know the margin. Let's say you earn 10% margin (profit), then on making a sale of ₹ 2000 throughout the day, your profit becomes 10% of it ie, ₹ 200. You have to set aside 10% of this sum of 200 that is, only ₹ 20.

"In this way, keep 10% aside from your daily income for the whole month. Let's say that at the end of the month, you have been able to keep aside ₹ 670, then you can start SIP of ₹ 600 per month and include the remaining 70 rupees in next month's savings."

Now Yogendraji said, "I don't get 10% margin on all the items of sale – on some I get a 2% margin, on some I get a 4, 6, 10, or a 15% margin. So, I never know what my monthly income is."

I told him that even if he assumed the average of 5% on all of these, he could assume a minimum profit of ₹ 100 on a sale of ₹ 2000. He could then start an SIP with ₹ 10 per day. But he laughed saying, "Nothing will happen with ten rupees sir."

He did not heed my advice and I feel very sad to see him in the same condition even after 3 years. Overall, if you are also an illogical person and you are not ready to accept financial discipline under any circumstances, then please stop reading this book. No book can help one who is not willing to help himself,

Sai Baba of Shirdi had said on one occasion that if you do not put into practice what you learn after reading books, then there is no use of reading books.

Therefore, my only request to you is to try adopting financial discipline of investing in an SIP by saving equal to 10% of your monthly income if not more. Then in 6 months you will start seeing a lot of benefit from this habit.

4. Now suppose, your monthly income was ₹ 5,000 and you started an SIP of ₹ 500 per month. Over time, as

your income increases, you can increase the amount of SIP. Your income after 5 years was 22,000 per month. Your monthly SIP of your savings (2200) is ongoing on and your savings amount has increased to 88,750 in 5 years. Now out of this savings, say you want to buy a motorcycle for ₹ 68,000. What would you do?

You will remember that in the beginning I wrote that 'be your own bank' in creating this method. I also call it method, but it does not mean that you bring a motorcycle by paying 68,000 units out of this SIP, bringing your balance to 20,750 and you continue with the SIP. I repeat again that becoming your own bank does not mean that you sell units and buy a motorcycle and have fun.

Suppose you didn't have an SIP and what would have happened if you had taken a motorcycle loan from the bank on finance? You would have had to put 20% of the amount in cash from your own pocket. That is, if you had 14,000 in cash, the bank would have given you a finance of ₹ 54,000. On that too, after taking a 10% monthly interest, it would have charged an installment of approximately 2,600 to 3,000 per month with interest in two years. So, here becoming your own bank means that you do not need margin money at all, even if you consider your own bank loan amount of ₹ 68,000. Now the SIP of 10% of your monthly income is 2,200. But also add to this the 10% loan repayment amount of ₹ 2,200 till you repay the entire 68,000 without interest. That is, now you have to maintain an SIP of 4,400 per month, in which the income which increases by 10 % of your monthly income of 2,200 will increase and the remaining 2,200 is the installment of your loan. After the entire 68,000 is paid back, you can discontinue this installment and continue with the SIP of only 10% of the monthly income. With this, after 5 years, your fund will grow more and more as your monthly income increases so that you will now be able to take a loan to buy a plot from it. There will also be an advantage. If you take a loan from the bank, then you have to pay interest, too. But here you do not have to pay interest along with getting the loan sanctioned immediately. Along with it profit booking takes place when needed as well.

## Summary

1. Save 10% of your monthly income and invest it in an SIP.
2. With this, along with increasing the income, the SIP amount will also increase automatically.
3. Take a loan from this fund as and when required so that profit booking will be done from time to time.

4. Recharge the loan taken without interest from 10% of the principal amount in addition to the monthly income.

5. This discipline will work wonders. Within a few years, you will have a very good corpus.

❑

# 13

# Financial Indiscipline

Recently a new computer operator, Nitin Vaishnav, came to me for work. I have the habit of giving advice without being asked to. I started giving financial tips to him as well. When he showed some interest, I presented *The Richest Man of Babylon* to him.

My thoughts were clear. I wanted him to learn to save 10% of his monthly income from the time he had just started his career. I told him that when he has at least ₹ 5,000 deposited by this method, then he can open his Demat account so that he can earn some money from swing trading in blue-chip shares and also get an SIP.

According to my estimate, it was going to take him at least 6-7 months to deposit the amount of ₹ 5,000. But he told me within 2 months that he had deposited 5,000, and he was ready to open the account. I was surprised. If I were to consider his salary, if he saved 10% of his monthly income, then it was impossible to save 5,000 in 2 months. That's why I asked him if he had any other source of income. He laughed saying, "Sir, I didn't save 10%. Since I am not married, instead of 10% I took out 5,000 directly from the salary."

I explained to him that this was a type of financial indiscipline and that it was completely wrong. If he wanted to take the right advantage of my method, then he had to neither save one rupee less than 10% nor a rupee more. Actually, this system is not based on savings at all.

Here, as soon as the salary is received, 10% should be kept aside thinking that it is not a part of the salary. For example, if someone receives a salary of 8,000 per month, then 800 rupees have to be set aside from it assuming that it is not part of the salary and that only remaining 7,200 is one's salary. If you want, you can spend it or save it. That means ₹ 800 which has already been deducted is not a part of either your income and savings. In a way, that amount is your employee who will earn on your behalf to make you rich.

If instead of relying on the method of first deducting money for the future and then spending it, you keep waiting for your savings. During some months you will save more and during others you will not be able to save at all. So, understand the essence of this 10% method and as soon as you get the money, put the first 10% aside to work for yourself. Make both your living and saving with the remaining 90%.

## Summary

1. Do not try to invest in an SIP by saving more than the prescribed limit. I do not forbid saving more than 10%. But don't consider saving 10% as an investment for yourself. Whatever you save extra, you can use to fulfil your future needs.
2. The amount invested in an SIP is like having employees who work for you.
3. As soon as the money is received, the amount should be deducted from it and invested in an SIP for a bright future. The remaining amount should be used for both running monthly expenses and savings. However, if the savings fall short, you can take an interest free loan from the SIP fund as mentioned earlier. But it needs to be recharged so that this fund keeps on growing.

❑

# 14

# Smart Averaging Method of Investing-cum-Trading in ETFs

My old followers know that I have not always been a supporter of the principle of 'Invest and forget' as the habit of locking your profits from time to time can protect your profits earned on investments.

If you do not book profits from time to time, then in case of sudden big drops in the market, your entire profit disappears and your portfolio will incur a loss. Then nothing remains in your hands. Investments have had such experience in 1993, 2001, 2008, 2018, 2020. So, booking profits on time is a practice that must be followed.

After doing a lot of research, I have prepared a combination of investing and trading in ETFs. This is what I call the Smart Averaging Method. I have designed it in such a way that only if the luck is very bad then there will be a loss. The rest of its risk-reward ratio remains mostly in favour.

Let me explain this method in detail:

In this, first divide your total amount into 10 parts. Suppose, you want to invest 3 lakh rupees in ETF trading investment by this method or you have 3 lakh rupees for trading then divide it into 10 parts ie, 30,000 a part.

I have mentioned 10 high-volume ETFs in the previous chapters of this book. But they are not final. To learn whether you need to go to the NSE or not, you sort out the high-volume ETFs yourself according to the method explained in my YouTube videos. You may keep checking the updated list on my channel as well.

It is not a necessary condition that you follow this method only in the case of these 10 ETFs. I have evolved thc method in a scientific way. If you want, you can choose any 10 ETFs of your choice. Just make sure they don't have too little volume. So, keep in mind that at least a volume of 1,000 is traded daily.

Also, keep in mind that these 10 ETFs are based on different sectors, such as:

1. Nifty 50
2. Bank Nifty

3. CPSE Index
4. Nifty IT
5. Nifty Next 50
6. Nasdaq
7. Nifty 100
8. BSE 500.

Thus, at least 10 ETFs based on different underlying assets can be taken care of.

Now if you want to invest ₹ 30,000 in an ETF, then for this also you have to make 6 parts of 5,000 each. From the first 5,000, you can create positions in all 10 ETFs at any level. Now you will have 2 options. If your ETF of 5,000 increases by 4.5% from your purchase price, you can book a profit. Otherwise, you wait. If the unit you bought turns into a loss of 5% before you get a profit of 4.5%, then you can average by buying another 5,000 units. Now you have an investment of ₹ 10,000 after averaging. You had to invest a maximum of ₹ 30,000 in an ETF. So, you still have a backup cash of 20,000 with you.

Now after averaging the profit target, reduce it by 0.5%. Now put a hold on the unit of 10,000 waiting for a 4% profit. If profit is not received and the unit falls further, then you have to do the next average after 10% fall from the average price (Note here that do not average after the first buy price has fallen by 10%. Here, after falling 10% from whatever average price came after the first average, the second average has to be done. Now the target of profit is to be reduced again to 3.5%). A detailed example of this method is as follows:

1. While making the first investment, let's say the price is ₹ 100, then you will take 50 shares for 5,000 and expect to earn ₹ 225 from the target of 4.5% profit.

2. Unfortunately the ETF fell 5% from 100 to 95. So, you made a new investment of 5,000 and took 53 new shares at a price of 95. You now have a total of 103 shares. Average Price Previously Buy Price 5,000+ Now 5,035 Total Investment 10,035 Divided by 103 will get 97.42.

   Now next time you have to average this 97.42 after falling 10%, that is, 87.68. Now your investment will be around 15,033 and with the addition of 57 shares, the total becomes 160 shares.

   Now you have to pay the target 3.5% only. That is, when there was an investment of 5,000, then the target of 4.5% was expected to generate an income of 225. If the investment is 10,000, then targeted 4%, now, the income of 400 is expected. If the investment is 15,000, then the target was again reduced by 0.5% to 3.5%, now the income of 525 is expected.

3. The next average is the average price of your average so far, which will be divided by 160 in 15,033 i.e.

after 15% fall of 93.95. You will not need to do much multiplication/division to find the average. Simply the broker in which you have taken the ETF will also show the average price, along with the percentage drop from the average.

4. After this type of averaging, the total investment amount will become 20,000 and the profit will again be reduced by half a percentage to 3%, that is, only ₹ 600.

5. Now the next average will be on a fall of 20% from the average price so far. You seldom have to come to such a position. Before that the target of 3% will be met. But if it has to be done, the target will be 2.5%. 25,000 would have been invested by now, 2.5% of it is 625.

   You must be wondering what is the point of reducing the target after each average? The rationale for this is very simple, that if one leaves with less percentage of profit due to increase in the investment amount, then the principal amount will be returned, which by investing in another ETF will again be able to earn for the target of 4.5%. Also, the ETF which is falling continuously, will get a chance to exit even if there is a slight bounce back.

6. The closing average will be 25% below the average purchase price. In this situation, the target will be

only 2%. But what if there is no profit even after this?

So, you will have a maximum block of ₹ 30,000, which is invested at different levels and not at the same time and the ETF is not a single stock, which may or may not grow. An ETF is a portfolio where some companies will grow as well. Whenever the market recovers, you will definitely get a chance to exit with a profit of 2%.

Therefore, this method of smart averaging is quite safe. If there is a big calamity like a war or any kind of a financial emergency, in which all the banks and financial institutions are ruined, even at times when your investment will sink. Otherwise, there are more chances of getting benefits from it. That is, in the language of the stock market, the risk reward ratio is in your favour only.

## Summary

1. In the smart averaging method, 5%, 10%, 15% 20%, 25% fall from the average price of purchase is averaged a maximum of 6 times, ie, original purchase once. After doing this 5 more times, the amount of averaging fund is noted, which can be bought for a maximum of 6 times.

2. Always remember here not to average after falling 5,10,15,20 and 25% from the original purchase

price for the first time. You will get the average price after averaging each time, The average after it falls 5,10,15,20 and 25%.

3. Whether the stocks will bounce back by averaging the falling stocks is uncertain. As the share of Yes Bank was part of Nifty and started falling from around ₹ 400 then it eventually came down to ₹ 6. In this, whoever did the average continuously by any method, got stuck. But this cannot happen in ETFs because ETF is not a single share but a basket of shares. Hence the rise in stocks is uncertain and it is not advisable to average out the falling stocks.

4. Since ETFs are a complete portfolio, there is no harm in averaging down a falling ETF though. However, do not average more than 5 times maximum because if your ETF is not able to give even 2% return even after averaging 5 times, then there is something wrong. After that it is better to stop the average and limit any potential losses from that.

5. With each average, the profit margin is to be reduced by half a percentage, which will be reduced from 4.5% to 2% after 5 averages.

6. Use the smart averaging method only in the 10 ETFs with the highest volume. This makes it convenient to buy and sell.

7. A question arises– If we keep 5 times the backup amount for an ETF, then will this amount will remain unusable and there will be no return on it? Therefore, this method is useless. The answer is that you keep the backup amount in Sovereign Gold Bond and Corporate Bond Funds, which will continue to earn returns and you can sell them anytime and get the amount. You have already read about them in this book.

❑

# 15

# SIP in ETFs

Many times, I am also asked about how to start an SIP in ETFs. Some investors do not want to trade in ETFs. They have personal compulsions. Some may not have enough time to manage the portfolio this way. Such investors just want to forget by starting an SIP in some big ETFs like mutual funds.

Currently, some brokerage companies in India offer the facility of SIP in stocks like mutual funds which is called Systematic Equity Plan. Since ETFs are treated against stocks, you can make an SIP in ETFs with this Systematic Equity Plan. But if your broker company or your online trading platform is not providing such a facility then the only option left with you is to manually buy a certain amount of ETF on a certain date of the month and start an SIP in it.

The biggest advantage we get in an SIP is that we do not need to invest much time and put in much mental effort. SIP is such a tried and tested disciplined method attested by all the economists over the years, in which the return is almost certain over a period of time.

## Summary

1. Like mutual funds, you can also start an SIP in ETFs.
2. SIP is the simplest, most disciplined way of investing, which is almost certain to yield returns in the long run.
3. If your broker does not offer an SIP facility in ETFs, then you can do the same manually.

❑

16

# Drop in the value of your SIP

I have met many investors who, inspired by the previous examples, start SIPs in mutual funds with great enthusiasm. But unfortunately, if there is a decline in the market while running SIPs for a short period of 1 or 2 years, and if they see a loss of 10 to 20% in their SIP, they start to panic.

Such investors take 2 big steps when they panic:

1. They further stop investing new money in the SIP, that is, stop the SIP because they cannot see the loss of their capital every day.
2. On seeing a 10 to 20% loss every day in the remaining mutual fund units, they keep getting sad. Then as soon as the market climbs up even a little bit

and their loss is made up, they very smartly walk out with a loss of only 50 to 100 rupees.

After this they say goodbye to mutual funds forever. After 4-5 years when the market goes up wildly, they accept the mistake and think that if they had not closed the SIP, then today they would have made a lot of profit. So, they repeat the same mistake once again. They start a new SIP again at a time when the stock market is operating at its highest levels. Shortly after the market falls, they think that maybe they did not choose the right fund.

In fact, sometimes when the market falls, your portfolio's fall is a kind of a paper fall because until you book the loss, it is only visible to you on paper and this loss is not a real loss.

You should generally not book profit or loss in SIPs before 9 years so that long term SIPs can easily absorb small and big swings in between.

Nevertheless, for those who want to book profits continuously, the method of selling 1% of the fund value has already been discussed in this book. In the next chapter, you will be told the method of planting a money tree. It has been described at length in my book *How to plant a Money Tree from Option Trading*. But in this book, I am going to tell you the erudite part of that method only for mutual funds so that even those who do not trade in options can enjoy the income tax free fruits by planting a money tree with this method.

## Summary

1. Try a lifelong SIP using my two methods with an automatic system with consistent profit booking.
2. With this, you will also get income tax-free income throughout your life and your net worth will also continue to grow. One of these methods is to sell a percentage of the fund value every month, you have read about in the previous chapters. You will read the description of the second method, the money tree, in the next chapter.

❑

# 17

# Planting a Money Tree

You must have thought many times how great it would be if money grew on trees. In your childhood, fed up with your extravagance, your parents must have chided you many times – "Money does not grow on trees!"

I'll teach you to plant such a tree, which will bear fruits from time to time and you will be able to get regular income by taking the fruits as per your requirement. Won't that make it worthwhile to read this book? I will also receive your 5-star review on my book as *gurudakshina.*

In this chapter, I am going to teach you how to plant a money tree with the help of Nifty ETF and Bank Nifty ETF, so that both your investment and profit booking will be disciplined in such a way that you cannot even imagine. You can use the money tree method in any ETF of your choice.

The biggest feature of this system is that you will not have to pay any income tax on the profits booked after 1 year. But if your tree bears fruit even before 1 year, then you will have to pay nominal income tax on the booked profit before this one year also. It will be less than 0.50%, whereas normally you have to pay short term capital gains tax at the rate of 15% if you book profit before 1 year.

Usually when you plant a tree, it starts bearing fruit in 3 to 7 years. This tree of mine starts bearing fruit in 1 week to 3 months. But you should start plucking the fruits only after 1 year to take advantage of the exemption of Long-Term Capital Gains Tax.

In this method, you have to choose a large ETF based on Nifty such as Nifty Seed, SBI Nifty ETF or Kotak Nifty ETF or any other which has a higher volume.

First of all, decide how much amount you have to invest in growing your money tree every month. If you want to invest 20,000 per month then divide this amount by 4. Now like you start an SIP in any mutual fund, you have to invest 5,000 in Nifty Seeds/Nifty ETFs on that day by making a schedule every week.

Say, you have fixed Friday for this auspicious work. This is called auspicious work because if you have understood the money tree and you have decided that you will leave trading etc. Believe me, this step of yours will change your life and you will continue to get such tax free regular income from the stock market that you cannot even imagine.

This method was first described in my book *How to Plant a Money Tree with Options Trading*, which has become India's bestseller book on options trading today. From time to time I keep getting e-mails from followers who planted such a tree from this book, in which they have described their earnings of lakhs of rupees.

So, if you have fixed Friday then you can buy shares of Nifty ETF for ₹ 2,000, 5,000, 10,000, 15,000 or as much as is comfortable for you on Friday and you can easily invest that amount every week.

Now it is your choice whether you buy it with limit order or buy it at any time in the current market. There is no need to put much thought in it, you can buy them at any time at any price.

To help you understand it easily, I will explain the whole story of my money tree to you with the help of old data. For this, I have used the data of Nifty Seed ETF from 5$^{th}$ May 2017 to 9$^{th}$ August 2018. When I explain the story with practical examples, you will be easily convinced and will absorb its facts.

Now 5$^{th}$ May 2017 was Friday. You can see the price data of Nifty Seeds from 5$^{th}$ May, 2017 to 11$^{th}$ May, 2017 in this table-

| Date | Open | High | Low | Prevcolse | ITP | Close |
|---|---|---|---|---|---|---|
| 05 May, 17 | 957 | 957 | 947.5 | 955.64 | 949.3 | 949.02 |
| 08 May, 17 | 955 | 955 | 949.58 | 949.02 | 950.75 | 950.27 |
| 09 May, 17 | 955 | 955 | 950.25 | 950.27 | 951.25 | 951.12 |
| 10 May, 17 | 953 | 960.7 | 952.51 | 951.12 | 960.7 | 960.03 |
| 11 May, 17 | 963 | 964.79 | 960 | 960.03 | 961.72 | 961.13 |

To explain to you, I have assumed that you buy or sell shares at the close price. For those who do not know the difference between close price and LTP (Last Trading Price) let me explain that the average price of any trade that happens half an hour before the close of the market is called close price. On the other hand, LTP is the price at which the last trade takes place.

So, we will assume that we are buying shares every Friday at the close price, ie, at a price during the last half hour of the market. If you have to invest 5,000, then at the close price of 949.02 on 5th May, 2017, you would have bought about 5 shares and your investment would have been ₹ 4,745.10. For the sake of simplicity in calculation, I have not included other expenses like brokerage, GST, STT, etc.

Now we will continue to look at the market value of our held shares from the daily close price, how much is the profit from our basic investment. Whenever we get profit more than ₹ 1,000 on our basic investment, then we will book profit by selling only as many shares, out of which only profit above ₹ 1,000 is available.

To understand, now see our profit and loss on the market value of 5 of our shares from 5th May, 2017 to 11th May, 2017 at the closing price of ₹ 4,745.10 in this table:

| Date | Close | Total Share | Market Value at Close | Basic Investment Value | Profit Loss |
|---|---|---|---|---|---|
| 05 May, 17 | 949.02 | 5 | 4745.1 | 4745.1 | 0 |
| 08 May, 17 | 950.27 | 5 | 4751.35 | 4745.1 | 6.25 |
| 09 May, 17 | 951.12 | 5 | 4755.6 | 4745.1 | 10.5 |
| 10 May, 17 | 960.03 | 5 | 4800.15 | 4745.1 | 55.05 |
| 11 May, 17 | 961.13 | 5 | 4805.65 | 4745.1 | 60.55 |

Now since we had a profit of only ₹ 60.55 on our original investment as on 11th May, 2017, we did not make any profit booking because whenever we get profit above ₹ 1,000 on our basic investment, only then we will book profit. We will start our weekly SIP as long as there is profit or loss less than ₹ 1,000, ie, every week we will continue to buy units at the market price by investing 5,000 in the last 30 minutes of market close on Friday.

## But what is the basic condition in this?

The basic condition will be that we will never calculate the average price, nor calculate the average price. We will then see what our basic investment is ie, Basic Investment Value. For this, you can also maintain a separate excel sheet. We will always calculate profit and loss on our basic investment only.

Like next week we again took nifty seeds of 5,000. Thus, taking every week we finally had 50 shares on 10th July, 2017. Then at the close of 10th July, 2017 we were making a profit of ₹ 1,245.70 in total, which was more than ₹ 1,000 profit. I have made a complete table of its 15 months' data. But it is not possible to publish the entire table as an e-book. That's why I am giving you its link in Google Drive. Before reading the book further, you should download or take a print out of the PDF of this table or at least keep it on the mobile in such a position that you can understand the examples of the book by looking at this table. The link of the PDF of the table is given below:

https://drive.google.com/file/d/1l0NqTCdnIjn0TABkxS5IJCxSZcvDekVI/view?usp=sharing

You have noticed that on 10th July, 2017 we were earning a net profit of ₹ 1,245.70 on our basic investment amount. Now we have to remove this profit of ₹ 1,245.70 from the market. For this, we will sell only 1 unit the next day on 11th July, 2017 by placing a limit order at the close price of 10th July at 1,008.18 because if we sell 2 units then profit booking will exceed 1,245.70. So, I will sell only 1 share.

Now we have taken out ₹ 1,008.18 from it assuming that we have taken profit only, that is, we have plucked the first fruit of our tree.

Now we are left with 49 shares. In the 50 shares that we had bought, our original investment was 48,763.30. Do not dilute this original investment. We still believe that this is our original investment. We have taken ₹ 1,008.18 out of profit, that is, only the fruit has been plucked – the original tree remains as it is.

So, now while calculating the profit above ₹ 1,000, we have to consider our original investment as 48,763.30 and every new unit we buy, we have to add this investment to this original investment and calculate 1,000 profit on it.

## What was the benefit of this?

The first advantage is that we know that we have withdrawn ₹ 1008.18 from profit, that too in just 2 months 5 days. But it is not your profit as per income tax rules. You have sold a share whose average purchase price was ₹ 975.26, which you sold for ₹ 1,008.18. So, as per Income Tax rules you have booked profit of only ₹ 32.92 out of which brokerage, STT, GST, delivery charges will be around ₹ 20. So, you have taken total profit of ₹ 13, of which 15% short term capital gains tax will be ₹ 1.95. That is, you will have to pay only 1.95 income tax of 1,008.18 profit, which is approximately 0.20%. Similarly, if you sell any share after this tree is more than a year old, then your tax liability on long term capital gains up to a profit of 1 lakh will become zero if it is considered to have been sold 1 year ago.

Now look at the data of the entire 15 months together to see how and when to sell only that many shares that only take profit, while the rest of the principal amount remains in the market. The link of the PDF of the table is given below-

https://drive.google.com/file/d/1l0NqTCdnIjn0TABkxS5IJCxSZcvDekVI/view?usp=sharing

Thus in 15 months we made an original investment of ₹ 3,35,420.70 by buying 5,000 Nifty seeds per week. But whenever the profit exceeded 1,000, we sold so many shares that the profit amount was earned. So, we also booked a total profit of ₹ 40,385.48 from this tree in these 15 months, which is approximately 12% profit of the original investment. This profit booking was also almost income tax free because after 1 year whoever sold one or two units, their profit was tax free.

Now consider a possible problem you have in mind. Probably some of my readers will also be there who will check the current market price of Nifty Seeds. So, it will look approximately ₹ 100, which may give them a big shock. How could this ETF break down from 1,193 and came straight to ₹ 100?

In fact, the Nifty seed did a face value split. Earlier its value was 1/10 of Nifty, which has now been reduced to 1/100. That is, later on the 282 shares which were still held, 10 shares were given instead of 1 share, which became

2820 shares of 282 and the value also became 1/10. That is, you'll have to understand that what you see as today's value of ₹ 100, you must consider it as ₹ 1,000 at that time.

That is, if you find the importance of keeping this profit booking less in the data of these 15 months, then remember, in March 2020, the price of Nifty seed went up to ₹ 142.95. By then how much profit would we have booked? Similarly, during the fall, on 23rd March 2020, its value was reduced to only ₹ 81. After that, the unit of Nifty seed increased again to ₹ 100 in May 2020. That is, if you had started this system, then your units would also keep growing and in any market situation your profit booking would also continue completely tax free because after 1 year you would have shares available to sell for long term capital gains.

By doing this, when you would have come down to 7,500 shares, then you would be in a position to book a profit of 7,500 if the Nifty seed price increases by Re 1.

With the help of this tree, you can earn money continuously in options trading also, the method of which I have described in *How to make Money Tree with Options Trading*. Also, remember that instead of putting all the money in one ETF, we can also plant trees in 5 or 10 different ETFs with the highest volume.

## A doubt and its solution

A follower of mine asked me that I have said that if the profit is more than ₹ 1,000, then the next day, take out that profit by selling the shares of the ETF. Accordingly, in the table I made, I have booked profit by selling one share for 1,008.18, seeing a total profit of 1,245.70.

But I have booked only a real profit of 32.92, in which I earned only 13 rupees by reducing STT and brokerage etc. This is your real profit of ₹ 13 and not ₹ 1,008.18. (1,008.18 is your sell price of one share. How did you calculate your profit?) That means I made a total profit of 13 on my original investment of 975.26. It earned only 1.3%.

According to this calculation, in the entire 15 months I sold shares of sale value of 40385.48 on the original investment of 3,35,420.70. But this 40,385.48 is not my real profit. Of these, my actual profit will be 4,400 less the original cost price of the share (approximately 36,000). When there was a profit of 4,400 on the original investment of 3,35,420.70, then again I got a profit of 1.3% in total. Don't you think a profit of 1.3% in 15 months is very low?

My answer to that follower was that this was the wonder of this method. In this, as we can see that we have booked a profit of 13 from the income tax rules. So, we had to pay negligible or no income tax on it. But actually, we did not reduce the original investment amount by even one rupee in our sheet. According to you, if we had made a profit of 13, then we would have reduced the original investment amount for each share we sold. But we did not reduce the original investment amount while calculating further, that is, at what value we have been buying and selling shares, they are not taken into account. Our main focus is on the tree. That is, there are two issues:

1. What is our original investment?
2. What is our profit on that investment?

For example, suppose the original investment is 100 and now its value at market price is 110. So, if we take out ₹ 10 out of 110, the original investment remains 100. Now it's a different question as to how to withdraw the 10 rupees. But if the original investment is not reduced, then by the rules of science and mathematics, what is the profit of the 10 rupees that you take out?

Actually, this method is based on amazing science. By not reducing the original investment in this, the profit of ₹ 1,008 that we booked was booked out of that one unit or share, which we have sold. But the remaining 1,008-13 = ₹ 995 has been booked from the remaining shares, due to which their average purchase price has increased in that proportion. So, the original investment is not reduced.

Hope, you must have understood that if we do not reduce the original investment then whatever increase there is in the original investment, will be profit. Selling out that profit by selling the units will reduce the number of units, but the average value of the remaining units or shares will increase in the same proportion that it will come in profit further only when this previous profit is met.

Thus, this money tree is truly wonderful. It has only two drawbacks. One drawback is that in this, you have to make an excel sheet and calculate the original investment and profit separately. You might not want to do the 5 minutes of hard work that is required every day.

The second drawback is that due to the fully automatic system, now you may not get the cricket-like thrill of trading every day by buying and holding the stocks that make you very rich.

❑

# 18

# Discount Method of Trading ETFs

Instead of trading in shares, the trend of investors in Indian stock markets in ETF trading is increasing. Recently, investors saw that the shares of some big companies like Yes Bank, India Bulls Housing Finance continued to fall, while all these companies came in the blue-chip category and were also part of the Nifty 50 index.

The massive 90% fall in the shares of the said companies taught investors that trading in blue-chip stocks is also not as safe as it was believed. In such a situation, the trend of investors is moving towards trading in the entire basket of shares instead of any one share. ETFs ie, Exchange Traded Funds Baskets are of similar stocks. Each ETF is a complete portfolio of 20, 30, 50, 100, 150 or sometimes up to 500 stocks.

Most ETFs are based on one or the other index, like all 50 stocks in the Nifty Seed ETF are in the same ratio as the Nifty. After the above initial information about ETFs, let me give you complete information about the discount method. The value of each ETF is based on two factors:

1. Own NAV (Net Asset Value) of ETF: Since ETF is similar to a mutual fund, so as a NAV of a mutual fund, ETF also has a NAV based on market value of underlying index of ETF. As Bank Seed is an ETF, its value of 1 unit is 1/100 of Bank Nifty. If you buy 100 units of bank seed (100 shares of bank seed) then 1 bank nifty index is equal to buy. Now if the market value of Bank Nifty is 29,670 then in theory, the NAV of Bank based Bank Seed ETF based on 1/100 of Bank Seed ETF stood at 296.70.

2. Since ETFs trade like stocks, the other factor in determining their valuation apart from NAV is their premium, eg, even if the NAV of an ETF is 296.70, its market value can also be 306.70 if there is high demand during trading. Here the premium is ₹ 10. Similarly, if ETF buyers are low and sellers are high, then the premium can also be in minus. For example, if the premium becomes minus ₹ 6, then

you can also get an ETF with NAV of 296.70 for 290.70.

Now we have to keep this fact in mind that you can get ETFs above and below their NAV in market value as well.

When ETFs are trading above their NAV, it is called trading at premium and when ETFs are trading below their NAV, it is called trading at discount. Now to understand the method I want to explain, it is very important to understand what is the creation and redemption process in ETFs.

A large financial institution that has the ability to buy a lot is called an Authorized Participant or an AP. Every ETF has an authorized participant or AP. These authorized participants provide the ETF provider by buying (from the secondary market) the proportion of the company's shares in the underlying index of the ETF and the ETF provider issues units in exchange for these shares to the authorized participant. They offer mutual funds to convert mutual funds into exchange traded funds by making them available to the buyer in the market. This is called unit creation.

Thus, the basic function of APs or Authorized Participants is to buy from the stock market the shares that an ETF wants to hold. For example, Nifty Seed ETF is designed to track Nifty 50. So, AP will buy all the shares of Nifty 50 exactly in the ratio of Nifty 50 and give it to the ETF provider. In return, the ETF provider will give the same number of units of the ETF (considered 100 units of Nifty seed for 1 Nifty.) to the AP. This unit will give the AP at the NAV value irrespective of the market price of the Nifty seed. Suppose the market price of Nifty seed is moving at 102 while Nifty is at 9,900. So according to this, the NAV of Nifty seed is 1/100 of 9,900 ie, 99 only. So, the AP will be found at unit 99. Now the AP market price is moving to 102, then the unit obtained for 99 is free to sell to the buyer at 102 to make profit.

This process also goes in reverse. For example, Nifty is at 9,900. But the market price of Nifty seed is trading at a discount of 96 (according to 9,900 NAV is 99, then the price of 96 is the discount price). So, the AP can also perform the reverse process. He will buy units of ETF from the market at a price of 96 and will take the shares of Nifty in return by giving these units to the ETF provider. Due to the high market value of these Nifty shares, naturally the AP will also benefit by this and the process of making the ETF provider available by the AP by buying ETF units in the market and getting the underlying shares in return is called redemption.

Now you may ask, what are the benefits to the ETF provider in this process? Basically, this process of creation/ redemption helps in keeping the market price of the ETF in the market close to its fair value, ie, the NAV.

AP monitors the market price in ETFs. If there are more buyers of ETF units and fewer sellers, then the premium appears to be rising from the ETF's Fair Value (NAV), then the AP jumps in and buys shares from the market and gives them to the ETF provider and takes units of the ETF in return. It increases the supply by giving it to the buyer and helps in bringing it close to the fair value ie, NAV by reducing the market price.

Similarly, if the ETF starts trading at a discount, the AP helps in bringing the units of the ETF to NAV by increasing its market price and taking the shares in return by giving the units purchased to the ETF provider.

Each ETF is monitored by multiple APs and the process goes on. This helps in keeping the market price of the ETF around the NAV.

Now you will ask, why did I bore you with this story? This may benefit the AP, it may also benefit the ETF provider. But what is my benefit in this? It is possible that whatever has been explained so far, you may have not have understood it fully. But now everything will make sense. What you have learned so far is to take advantage of the discount method of buying ETFs.

Basically. every ETF has its iNAV ie, Intrade NAV or Indicative NAV available on its website. This iNAV is refreshed every 10 to 15 seconds so that the AP can continuously monitor the iNAV for unit creation and redemption.

Like you want to see the iNAV of Nippon India ETF'S, then you can search by typing Nippon India ETF iNAV on Google and go to the website of Nippon India ETF and watch live iNAV. Similarly, if you search by typing SBI ETF iNAV or ICICI ETF iNAV, you will be able to see live iNAV by visiting the website of SBI ETF or ICICI ETF.

Now you have to keep track of iNAV like AP. If the market price of this ETF is more than 2% below its iNAV, you can buy at a discount.

I know now you will say that you do not have enough time to constantly keep an eye on the market price of INAVs and ETFs. So, it doesn't matter. You have to check the NAV and market price of the top 20 ETFs with high volume every day when the market is about to close around 3 o'clock like AP. If the ETF is trading at a discount of more than 2% from its NAV (iNAV), then you have to buy it. With this, the very next day itself, you can easily leave with a target of 2 to 3%. How do you do that?

Let's say, the Intrade NAV or Indicative NAV of Nifty Seed at 3 pm is 93.36. But if you check, its market price may be many times, you can see it trading at a discount of 2% or more. That is, if the Nifty seed is at 91.40 at that time and you buy units of 4,000 to 5,000 of it, then the very next day after the market opens in the BTST segment, you will also want only 3% profit. So, 3% above 91.40 is only 94.14, which will not be very difficult to come and if you keep the target only 2%, then 2% above 91.40 is only 93.22, which can be easily found.

If not found, you can use the Smart Average Method mentioned earlier in this book.

If 2% is available in one day, then after deducting the cost of 1%, 1% will also be saved. So, you can also earn 20% in 20 trading sessions in a month. Suppose if you can earn only 10 days, then 10% month, that is 120% annually?

Trading in the stock market is always risky. These examples are given just because you don't find 2% return too low. In the rest of the method, even if instead of getting 2% return, we fall back, then we can use the safe averaging method mentioned in the previous chapters.

## Summary

1. ETFs also have the same NAV as mutual funds.
2. It is not necessary that based on 1/100 of Nifty like Nifty closed at 9875, then Nifty seed which is based on 1/100 of Nifty declares its NAV as 101.73. According to you it was 9,875, based on 1/100 it should have been 98.75. But sometimes this NAV can be more or less than this. There can be 2 reasons for this type of low/high NAV:

i. Dividend Factor

ii. Tracking Error

Here, due to the dividend of the holding companies by ETF, sometimes the NAV can be higher than that of the growth fund and the second reason is the tracking error. That is, due to the lack of coordination between the ETF provider and the AP as mentioned earlier in this chapter, the ETF may not be able to hold shares in the same ratio as the index. Therefore, at times the NAV of an ETF can be higher or lower than that of the index.

❑

# 19

# Investing in ETFs or Mutual Funds

Often, my followers ask me these questions:

"Sir, is it safe to invest in mutual funds?"

"Sir, is it safe to invest in ETFs?"

"Sir, is it safe to invest in such a mutual fund scheme or such an ETF?"

For this, we have to first understand the basic principle of the earth. What is the basic principle of the earth? You build a house using the best quality cement, and the strongest iron bars in the market. But many times, such strong buildings have been seen to be grounded in devastating earthquakes in many places of the world.

The *Titanic* was the safest ship. In it, complete security measures were taken with the technology of that time. The *Titanic* sank. Einstein had made a very important discovery; if that had come before the world today, I do not know what would have happened. But due to a sudden fire, that research was destroyed. It is said that the entire kingdom of Dwarka built by Lord Krishna was completely submerged in the sea. There are many such examples in the world.

A rabbit goes to drink water in the forest. While drinking water, he is very careful because at any time the predatory animals can catch him. A lion can also be hunted in the same way. So, what is the basic principle of the earth – 'Nothing is safe here.' You will say, "No, I do not believe that. My money in the bank is absolutely safe."

No, unfortunately it is not true. Many of the safest and biggest banks in the world have sunk. Washington Mutual Bank was the largest bankrupted bank in the US which went bankrupt in 2008. At that time, it employed 43,000 employees.

The Washington Mutual Bank had 2,200 branches which operated in 15 states. It had deposits of $188.3 billion. This bank was so secure that 60% of its business was retail banking, 20% was through credit cards and only 14% of house loans were given by it. Of all the loans that are available, the house loan is the most secured loan in which the house property is kept as a mortgage. But only

14% of these home loans drowned the entire bank because in the recession of 2008, no one was ready to buy a house of 10 million dollars even for 1 lakh dollars.

Now you will say, "Sir, never mind that even banks are not safe. But my investment in gold is absolutely safe." No, you can look up the topic on Google. Once aluminium was more valuable than gold. When Napoleon Bonaparte had guests, the guests of higher status ate in aluminium vessels and his petty servants ate in gold vessels.

Aluminium was more expensive than gold because a very small amount of aluminium was produced from aluminium ore. Later a scientist found a way to make cheaper and more aluminium from aluminium ore. After that, the prices of aluminium dropped so much that today you drink Pepsi in an aluminium can and throw it on the road. Tomorrow, if many gold mines are found somewhere or if scientists find some method of making gold like alchemists, then the price of gold can drop drastically.

Thus, my clear and unanimous opinion is that, 'nothing is safe on earth and anything can be destroyed by an 'act of God' or man-made calamity, scam, fraud, natural calamity. Still, we cannot stop living life. That's why you must have read and heard such disclosures like 'trading in stock market is very risky' or 'mutual fund investments are subject to market risk'.

❑

# 20

# Income Tax Rules on SIP

Another question may also come to your mind – how much income tax do I have to pay on the income from Mutual Funds/ETFs? Before answering this question, I want to tell you two important things.

1. The first thing is that the rules of income tax keep changing every year. The income tax rules mentioned in this book are with reference to 2020-21. Whenever you are reading this book later, make sure to verify the rules at that time by visiting the website of the Income Tax Department.

2. There is a famous American writer Robert Kiyosaki, who has written the book '*Rich Dad Poor Dad*'. He has also co-authored several books with the former US President Donald Trump. He wrote that the laws

that the governments make are mostly in favour of the rich because rich people donate to the governments and by influencing the rich governments, they get laws made in their favour in some way or the other.

Therefore, according to the books of Robert Kiyosaki, the income tax rules also remain as follows - If you are from middle class, then you may have to pay the highest tax, but if you belong to upper rich class then income tax laws can provide you relief from tax liability.

You must have understood that since investing in mutual funds is mostly done by upper class people, your tax liability in mutual funds is going to be much less as compared to the income from your job.

Now let us review the tax liability as per the current Income Tax Law. Share/Shares-based Mutual Funds/ Share-based ETFs - In all three, if you sell the shares before 1 year, you have to pay income tax at the rate of flat 15%.

Now if your income is less than minimum taxable income of 2.50 lakhs then you do not have to pay any tax. If your income from salary, business and other sources is 2.00 lakhs and short-term capital gain of 1 lakh (gain from shares, mutual funds, ETFs sold before 1 year is called short term capital gain) then your total income is 2 + 1 = 3 lakhs. In this, you have to pay 15% short term capital gain and 4% education cess on 0.50 lakh left after minimum income of 2.5 lakhs.

If your other income is 1.5 lakh and short-term capital gain is 1 lakh, then no tax is payable on it as total income is equal to minimum taxable income of 2.5 lakh. (Please verify any information by visiting the official website of the Income Tax Department. I have tried my best to give you the correct information from the latest rules at his discretion, but still you should take information about the latest circulars from the authorized website. Calculate your taxability as the rules keep changing from time to time).

Now you will ask, "How is this law in favour of the stock marketers?" If the income of the common man is only 5% in the middle of 5 lakhs, while the short-term capital gains tax will be 15%, then it is in favour of the employed.

But my dear readers, you can save this short-term capital gain. This is called income tax harvesting. Suppose you have received short term capital gain of 0.75 lakh from 1st April, 2019 to 29th March, 2020, then check such stocks/ ETF funds in your portfolio 5 minutes before market close on 30th March, 2020 who are running at a loss. You book a loss by selling them. As soon as the market opens the next day, these shares are bought back on 31st March, 2020, which will get you almost at the same price, from which these shares will be considered as newly bought. Tax liability will be calculated on these whenever you sell them.

The loss you booked was not an actual loss as your number of shares remained the same. You took back as many shares as you sold or took them back the next day.

(If you want, you can take back the shares as soon as you sell them. But some followers get confused by this. They say that it is intrade. But in reality, when you select CNC (cash and carry) in the product, it can't be intrade. But to satisfy such people, I have given the advice to buy as soon as the market opens the next day instead of buying back by hand.

That way you haven't really made any loss. But you can reduce this short-term loss booking from your short-term capital gains. For example, if you made a short-term capital gain of 0.75 lakh and booked a loss of only 0.75 lakh, then your net gain is zero and no tax is to be paid on it. If there is a gain of 0.75 lakh and you can book a loss of 0.25 lakh only, then on the remaining 0.50, you have to pay 15% short term gain and educational cess payable there

❑

# Epilogue

My dear readers, today I am very happy that the book which God made me write is finally complete. I was a mere instrument in this work. I hope that by taking advantage of the information given in this book, you will use all my methods with confidence and will definitely be successful in the direction of attaining financial stability and independence.

If you have benefitted from my book, then kindly give your 5-star review of the book. Almost 12 years of research in developing my methods and a year of writing has culminated in this book.

I am very happy when I read your reviews and also get inspiration to write more books.

I am overwhelmed to receive all your love and affection. I know that I will not be able to respond to all your comments and emails. But still, I try my best to answer as many YouTube comments and e-mails as possible.

❑❑❑